SOMEONE TO LOOK UP TO

A Lay View of Leadership

Rebekah Robinson

Text and cover design by Beckon Creative

Photographs courtesy of Michael Weavers,
Beckon Creative, and iStock

First published in Australia by
Beckon Creative © 2019
Brisbane, Australia
www.beckoncreative.biz/publishing

ISBN: 978-0-6486684-0-4

The author asserts the moral right to be identified as
the author of this work.

 A catalogue record for this book is available from the National Library of Australia

If you would like to read more by Rebekah Robinson,
see her *Faith Life Art* blog at
https://beckrblog.wordpress.com
and follow her Facebook page
Rebekah Robinson Author.

Rebekah's music album *Day In The Sun*
is available on iTunes and Spotify,
or in hard copy from beck@beckoncreative.biz

Contents

Foreword 4

1 Because I Said So 7

2 This Is the Way We've Always Done It 19

3 And What's Your Background ...? 27

4 The Big Picture 37

5 Just Like Jesus Used to Make 56

6 One Plus One Equals Three 71

7 Oil Change 92

8 Safe Kitchens 99

9 Eagles, Shields and Pedestals 114

10 And For My Next Trick ... 127

11 An Ounce of Prevention 145

12 Sharing Shoes 160

13 Words of Affirmation 175

References 181

Foreword

HI, AND WELCOME TO A BOOK on church leadership written by a non-leader! You may be wondering why on earth a lay person would summon up the audacity to tell a church leader how to do their job. The bulk of the leadership books I've seen on the shelves and web pages of Christian bookstores, are books written by leaders for leaders. The rationale is, "I've done it; here's how." I want to offer something different: feedback. I hold a Certificate of Christian Ministry and a Diploma of Youth Work, but I'm not a leader in the traditional sense. I don't have "leadership gifts", and I don't even *want* to be a leader. (I've led music teams, with middling results, but I'm more relational than dynamic. I mention this, and three decades to date of actively serving in church, lest you worry that you are reading the ramblings of an armchair critic.)

This book came about over lunch with a fellow abuse survivor, who questioned whether things would ever change in the hierarchy and culture of the church. I answered that things had improved, but that if we really wanted to see patterns change and abuse eradicated, we would have to change the way we taught leadership—because if we always do what we've always done, we'll always get what we've always got. I'm not sure how different today's leadership training actually is from that of 20 years ago. While I do see some welcome shifts, I also see some prevailing attitudes which give me pause.

So, if you're interested in unpacking a vision of what church leadership *could* look like, enjoy! I will be honest about the shortcomings I've seen, yet this is not an exposé, but rather an exploration. My ideas are untried, but at nearly 50, having been in church since birth, I've seen a lot of different leadership styles across three countries. I do have a few scars. I'm hoping you'll permit me to get some mileage out of them for the purpose of edifying the Church.

I'd like to thank the many excellent leaders I've had, and my beta readers for their input; my husband, Chris Robinson, and our kids, Daniel & Emma; my parents, Trevor & Kay Weavers and Heather & the late Lloyd Robinson; my amazing and supportive pastors; Anne Hamilton, who has mentored me through the authoring process; and Koda-Jo Berry Stewart, who inspired it.

Writing a book is a lot like writing a song: the notes have all been heard before, but one hopes that the combinations, arrangements, and actual voice will have a freshness. So here I go. You are beautiful people called to a difficult thing, and I honour you. Allow me to add to your store of market research just a little. As always, ask the Lord for guidance. If you like what I say, you are welcome to springboard off it. And if you don't, you can always tell yourself that this is just an opinion piece, which it is.

Rebekah Robinson
September 2019

1 Because I Said So

NOBODY CAN EVER GO INTO PARENTHOOD and come out unscathed. It's the leadership role that a huge chunk of us take on, whether we're gifted for it or not, and in some cases whether we desire it or not. If you are not a parent (and some of you won't be), you will at least have *had* parent figures of some stripe in your life at some point, so please don't groan too loudly just yet! Besides, the unique joy of discovering your limitations through child rearing may well be ahead of you in just a few short years, who knows.

I'm Gen X, as you may have guessed. I'm a wife, parent of two young adults, regular churchgoer, and sometime songleader; my stock level sits somewhere between "not a crackpot, can be a bit flaky, heart of gold" and "big on promise, short on delivery". I was once called a "velvet sledgehammer", but that's another story! We go on trying, don't we? And sometimes we are *very* trying …

My parents were missionaries, so I must disclose here that I do bring a certain amount of MK/PK experience to the table, and that may colour what I write. It also put me in much more regular, close-up contact with a range of leaders and leadership models. Everything colours what an author writes, anyhow. You'll see a lot of hues emanating from my New Zealand culture, my gender, and my denomination, as well as my generation.

The thing about being Generation X is that we were parented by Baby Boomers. And the thing about Boomers is that they were parented by Builders. This is going to mean different things to different people. I can speak of my own experience and observation, but you may find it parochial, so take it with a grain of salt.

Born in the early 1970s, I grew up with the certain knowledge that at the back of all adult dicta was *Because I Said So. And I Am Your Parent (or Teacher or Pastor or Policeman or Prime Minister). And So You Must Toe The Line.* Let's give this a shorter name, shall we? I shall christen it "the appeal to authority". This is what John C. Maxwell calls a "positional leader". It's not so much to do with the threat of consequences, though they do loom large behind the adult's shoulder. It's to do with *respect*. It says, "You owe me a measure of respect simply because I hold this position of authority in your life, and people in those positions are automatically granted honour and maybe even a bit of awe." So, it's not just an appeal to authority: it's also an appeal to the *dignity* of that authority.

> *It's not just an appeal to authority: it's also an appeal to the dignity of that authority.*

Generation X Christians in my circle might have dreamed of disobeying their parents, but they kept those dreams well tamped down. Verbal defiance was out of the question. Actually, most verbals were out of the question. Children were to be seen and not heard. Our Boomers, with the various maxims and anxieties handed down to them from their Builder parents, were light on extravagance and emotion, and heavy on steering the household into a place of modest prosperity. The fathers worked hard, assuming an Acts of Service love language whether they were born with it or not. The mothers kept up appearances. And it was important to have well-behaved, well-turned-out, thoroughly Christian-looking children. There was a lot of love. Large chunks of it were expressed through ensuring we were best placed to not make fools out of ourselves, our families, or our Saviour.

We were speaking of the dignity of authority. Various people in authority could at any time hand down a pronouncement you would have to abide by. Any pushback against that edict was tantamount to an attack on that person's dignity. It was like saying, "I don't respect you, I don't respect your office, I don't think you deserve your office, and I think that, in my vast experience, I know better than you do."

Imagine my shock to discover that this fear-of-the-Board was not the beginning of wisdom outside my church. My public school classmates didn't talk back to their teachers, but they didn't venerate them, either, and they had a low opinion of politicians and law enforcement. Imagine my further shock to discover that my own children, surprise surprise, weren't sold on the authoritative model. No amount of reiteration, illustration or verse-quoting brought enlightenment.

I recently worked as a primary school chaplain in an Australian state school for nine years, in addition to co-raising to my own two grown children. I therefore feel somewhat qualified to comment on the emerging generation. And what I've noticed is this: old models of leadership are not cutting it for today's kids. Those methods are tried—but they are no longer necessarily true across the board. It has nothing to do with the quality of our teachers, which is outstanding. It has nothing to do with their very reasonable expectation that children ought to do as they are told, for their own and the common good. It has to do with cultural evolution. And it has a lot to do with entitlement, but that's a far more complicated issue than most people give it credit for.

So let's talk about entitlement.

I feel that "entitlement" is a word simply bristling with porcupines. Nobody wants to be labelled "entitled". That would mean that scorn is being levelled at our guarding of something precious to us, as though it were not precious after all, or we were dummies to guard things or imagine ourselves worthy of them. Also, I think most people who point a finger at the "entitled" younger generations are generally doing it disparagingly. "Kids these days! They're so entitled!" But is *entitled* really another way of saying *they will unhesitatingly lay claim to things they have a right to?* Are we actually talking about a gap between the notion of rights and the notion of self-sacrifice?

> *Have we ever stopped to ask ourselves whether we are equally entitled?*

Have we ever stopped to ask ourselves whether we are equally entitled? The child in the classroom believes they have something worthwhile to say. The teacher believes the same thing about herself. The difference is that the teacher has been given a mandate to hold the floor, and the student has not. The student is not *less than* the teacher. The student is enrolled with an agreement that he or she has a defined role to play in the mini-society of school. It's when they want to push out of that role, or usurp someone else's role, that trouble ensues. So I submit to you the rocket-science idea that a rebellious pupil is simply one who is violating the agreement made between their parents and the school. And you can't help but see that this lack of personal agency is going to frustrate them at times. Church is much the same, except that no adult churchgoer wants to be dealt with as though they are five years old. You can turn up to church in good faith, only to be informed that your Heavenly Father has (apparently) gone over your head and made some rather dodgy arrangements with the Headpastor that you have no say in. Requests for clarification and documentation are not always welcome.

That's not quite true, actually, about not having a say. You always have a say with God. You just have to remember to say it, and to believe that if no cross-purpose prevents Him, He'll intervene in due course. And ideally, you should have a say in how you are treated in church.

Here's another piece of rocket science. The reason the current crop of children feels so entitled is perhaps that they have been raised to believe their voices matter. And this could be a natural by-product of many (not all) Gen X people being raised to believe that their voices *didn't*. As others have put it, parents tend to give their children what *they themselves* needed. The Builders lived through war and Depression, lacking plenty, and not wanting to discuss traumatic things. Some of them therefore drummed the need for frugality and the Cone of Silence into their Boomers. Those Boomers who then believed security and hard work were essential for success, put all that onto their Gen X children to help them succeed in life. Perhaps a lot of Gen Xers cried out for a separate self-esteem and room to express themselves because they had defined themselves by success or lack of it. At any rate, what I see now is a lot of Gen X parents frantically pouring self-esteem into Gen Z, whether it's in short supply or not. Gen Z, of course, does need self-esteem, as much as any generation does. What's in short supply for them now seems to be, among other things, community spirit. Compensate that too far in the subsequent generation, though, and you'll have a rigidity where it's not just "not all about you" but also "never ever about you".

Spiritual authority is a real thing. The Bible gives a lot of weight to obeying, supporting and honouring the leaders put above you—not just church leaders, but also worldly leaders, who (for reasons known only to Himself) God has permitted to carry a certain mantle. Even when said leaders are indifferent or evil, we are instructed to avoid reviling and to be obedient citizens. When it comes to leadership of God's people, He doesn't even like us to grumble. And I must confess, I've been an expert grumbler. Largely this has come about when I have permitted fear into my life. I have felt helpless in the arena of honest discourse, and resorted to venting outside of it. I have underrated God as my defender and advocate, and for all these things, I have needed to repent.

There is a place for seeking advice. Often the things we want to complain about are just in our heads; and for this reason it can be wise to get a second opinion before knocking on the pastor's door. Getting fourth and fifth and sixth opinions is less advisable. "White-anting"— when a complainant gathers like-minded grumblers and eats away at the credibility of the leader—is not a godly approach. The only person we should be "in cahoots with" is Jesus.

When the things we want to complain about are genuinely issues that need change, we must learn how to express ourselves not in terms of complaint but in terms of contribution to a viable solution. Matthew 5 outlines procedures for conflict resolution, and all of us are responsible for honouring it, whether conditions are ideal or not.

However, the leader also has a certain responsibility to *try* to create ideal conditions. They will need to practice active and open

---

Spiritual authority *is a real thing,
but so is the* circle of love.

listening, possibly with calming techniques, and always hand-in-hand with the Lord. Everything must be approached on both sides with love and respect. This is more difficult than it sounds. Yet if there is no open door and open ear, what relief can exist for those who are hurting under systems that need change?

Spiritual authority, as I said, is a real thing, something God takes seriously. But the circle of love the church was created to be—that also is a real thing. When the church looks less like one guy up the front and the rest in orderly rows facing him, and more like a community that eats and plays and shares together in a living room, we get closer to our origins. And in that scenario, the pastor is entitled to as much loving support as anyone else in the room. He becomes *someone we know and talk with,* rather than *someone who talks at us.* So when he outlines the way things are going to unfold in that community, he does so from inside it, knowing the names, challenges and potential of the people he's speaking to, willing to unpack thorny questions and allay anxieties. It doesn't have to be a democracy for everyone to feel heard. When people are known and listened to, they are far happier to invest their trust. The church is not an external construct that everyone must now fit into. It is a Body: not imposed from without, but growing and rising from within.

The Incarnation signalled a change in the way we relate to God. Suddenly, it was no longer, "Come to Me through your priest." Instead, it was "Come to Me: *I Am* your priest!" Once God Himself had taken a seat in our living room and broken bread with us and washed our feet, was there room any longer for a middleman to require reverence from us? And yet deference to one another is part of the Christian spirit. So then it becomes more a question of showing honour to everyone in the room—including our minister, who is a facilitator, not a roadblock. His job is not to be the *door* to God—nor the bouncer—but to be the *usher* who helps us find the door when we are unsure of it.

Don't mistake me here. I'm not defrocking the world. Denominations who still employ priests are not "doing it wrong," they are simply coming at it from a different angle. There is something very beautiful in the way they live out "confess your sins to each other and pray for each other so that you may be healed." (James 5:16) Having a person acknowledge your penitence and reinforce God's forgiveness is, indeed, very healing, provided that God is actually involved in the process and not peripheral to it. Probably the practice of repeating prayers was simply meant to help people receive and cement revelation in their hearts: "Meditate on this 'til it sinks in!"

The reverence these Christians give God by not treating His presence and favour as casual things, is precious alongside the confident intimacy with which others run into the Throne Room and throw themselves into Daddy's lap. There is room for both.

The Bible says three times that the fear of the Lord is the beginning of wisdom, yet it is predated by the greatest commandment, which is that we should love the Lord with all our heart, mind, soul and strength. If "the end of a matter is better than its beginning," could it be that while we *begin* gaining wisdom with fear—healthy dread, reverence, awe at His power and holiness—that we find wisdom's *culmination* in absolute love for and with God? Perfect love casts out fear, and the one who fears is not made perfect in love: they are still expecting God to hit them. The only one who has perfect love is God Himself. Why would He drive out fear from us, while simultaneously telling us we're stupid if we don't fear Him? I believe that the fear of God is the healthy place

---

The fear of the Lord is the beginning of wisdom, but love is at the other end of it.

---

to start, but it is not the place to finish. The end of the matter is to know that while God will continue through all eternity being terrifyingly awesome in power and holiness, this is something to be adored rather than run from. He is not only mighty, but altogether beautiful, and the things in Him that cause the nations and heavens to tremble are the very things that make Him our strong defender and show us the passionate outworking of His nature, Love. As we behold Him we see that He is *just* rather than punitive, and that He Himself has indeed paid all our debts. As we move closer to His likeness, our love for Him becomes less and less fearful, and more and more abandoned.

One more thing should be said about "because I said so". While Boomer parents did expect obedience mainly on the basis of their job description, it would be unfair to presume that they didn't have good reasons for commanding their children. When I became a parent, I realised that "because I said so" is really code for: "Yes, I have a valid reason for this decision. No, I don't have time to make it sound plausible to you. It would take a very roundabout lecture to explain my reasons, which neither of us has the time or energy for. In addition, I would need to reference extraneous facts that are too adult for you to manage. And I don't want to give you the dumbed-down version, because that'll just provide you with an opportunity to argue with me about its supposed merits. So please just trust in my judgment and my love for you, that I'm not being arbitrary about this—it really is for the good of you and us and everyone—and that it's important you comply even though you don't understand why."

There's a wry cowboy meme which goes, "If you get to thinkin' you're a person of some influence, try orderin' somebody else's dog around." The dog obeys its master because it loves him and is loved by him. In the same way, if you're going to be the kind of leader who hands out orders, you'll get a better response if the person you're addressing believes you love them, want the best for them, and always have their back in situations where you're privy to information that they're not. And if you *can* explain your rationale, do.

Occasionally you'll come across leaders in your life who will hand you a certain interpretation of a Bible passage and want you to blindly accept it "because I said so." Some of them will get quite huffy about it, adding that "this is what the Church has always believed." Has it? Everywhere? Always? Often what they are looking for is an acknowledgment that they have done their homework and we trust them, that they are part of a Correct Majority. They invite us to settle for a proxy relationship with the Word, through them. But what if they haven't done their homework? Or, what if they have, but their research didn't take them far enough, or far enough from their own confirmation bias? What if *their* pre-internet teachers didn't do *their* research? How would we know? What misery has been visited on God's people by the spreading of misinformation coming from poor translation across historical and cultural distance!

There is absolutely nothing wrong with people doing their own study into Bible interpretation, culture and history. While we may not be able to completely get inside the head of a prehistoric Middle Eastern herdsman, we can, at the very least, shake ourselves loose from a 21st-century Western mindset. And if we truly believe that God's Word is living and active, sharp and discerning, then it can stand a little robust prodding, can it not? Will not any serious Christ-surrendered student of the Word find themselves immersed in Him and coached by His Spirit? If anything, I would urge you to encourage believers to not only conduct their own investigations, but to investigate ruthlessly and without relent and from all angles. Be a noble Berean. Because if God's Word does not stand up under scrutiny, should we really be following it? Either it's the real deal, or it's not.

So, if the first website someone comes across is arguing that the Word cannot be infallible, tell them to keep investigating. Find all the other websites that refute the first one. Apply faith. Give more benefit of the doubt to people who love God, rather than people dedicated to opposing Him, because there *may* be more alliance with truth in that direction; but walk all around the problem and probe it. God can take it. It is not disrespectful to the founders of our faith; in fact, it honours them. And it makes our experience of the Living Word so much richer. At the moment I am researching the fruit of the Spirit for another book. I find those 7-12 concepts in Galatians so fascinating and so enmeshed— but if I had stopped at the English NIV, I would have missed a world of nuance that has caused me to fall in love with Jesus all over again.

Instead of squashing doubt in your parishioners until it dwindles to the size of an elephant in the room, allow us our doubts, and our hard questions. Be a safe place to talk about them freely and without condemnation or whitewashing. Answers are not as necessary as empathy. I believe all of us come to a place where we have to strip off the layers of Christian paint that have been plastered over our raw faith in Jesus. When we get to the bottom of it all, He is there; but let us not hamper the process by adding *more* unhelpful coats and a fake smile, asking people to toe the company line. Let people be honest. Don't require them to display a sanitised version of themselves in order to fit in. They get enough embossing from the world. We are here to facilitate *transforming* through the power of the Holy Spirit, rather than merely *conforming* through the social pressure of righteous community. You can't enlist to become a butterfly without showing up as a caterpillar. Love them while they hurt and ponder and blunder their way through

We are about transformation,
not conformation.

to authenticity. Jesus is love, and love rejoices in the truth. Overselling Christianity as something it's not, can do great harm. Life is lumpy, leaders are fallible, miracles are not as thick on the ground as we would like, and change takes time. The point is that Jesus is with us in it. What will He do next?

An intelligent person is defined as someone who can form their own opinions without leaning on the opinions of others, but is willing to change their opinions if better evidence is given. Examine the evidence for changes to Bible interpretation and church methods.

Talk to the Lord about these things. Take them to Him in earnest prayer. Ask the Holy Spirit to continually guide you into more truth. Let the transcendent peace of God guard your heart and mind as you seek.

2 This is the Way We've Always Done It

ONE OF THE BIG TRAPS in church life is to keep doing things simply because there's precedent.

I grew up in a wonderful Pentecostal church, but there were some things that were never explained that we all just ... went along with. One of these things was the dancing. (If you're from a church that doesn't hold with dancing, relax, I'm not selling it, just telling it.)

When congregational dancing occurred in our services in the 80s, it was a particular sort of dancing. And it tended to go with certain parts of certain songs. This little manoeuvre was defined for me later as "the Pentecostal Two-Step." It consisted of a tiny jump, a kick with the left foot, a hop back to ground zero, and a kick with the right foot; lather, rinse, repeat. It was a little like skipping solemnly without a rope, or doing the Riverdance without the uilleann pipes. I thought there must have been something really spiritually significant about this particular step, because it was the only congregational dancing I ever observed in our church. It was performed on the spot, in the rows, with an immense amount of glad dignity, even suppressed excitement. The unspoken rule was, "If you're one of the Really Spiritual Ones™, when you get to the chorus in this song—only the chorus, and only this

This is the Way We've Always Done It

song—you'll be observed doing this dance, and only this dance." And so we all carefully copied our Really Spiritual elders, and did this move on cue even though we felt ridiculous doing it (Gen X liked to pogo, not two-step). We teenagers frantically hoped this wasn't the moment someone we knew from school had decided to pop in. And if I felt embarrassed, I was less embarrassed that I disliked the two-step and more embarrassed because obviously my embarrassment revealed that I was ashamed of church ways, and therefore by extension, ashamed of the gospel, because wasn't it all of a piece?

And so here we have a situation where something that no doubt originated in a genuine, joyful personal response to God by some fellow somewhere in the 1960s, turned into something that made people in the 1980s feel foolish, ashamed, scripted, judged, and out of breath. It actually distracted me from God, because it dumped a load of mental and emotional steps on me that I had just sixteen bars to get through before the chorus descended. I dreaded that handful of "dancing songs" and the loadedness of the situation. My options were to look rebellious, look unspiritual, or look silly. And the last thing our church leaders—good people whom I still love and respect—would have wanted was to put all that on us. They would have been hoping for genuine joy in the Spirit. It's just that they had standards for what that joy looked like, and we weren't questioning authority, so nothing changed. What actually happened in practice was that we were being asked to duplicate a method that worked for someone else, in the hope or the assumption that it would work for us, too. But it was all backwards. It was not that joy rose up in us and we couldn't help but dance. It was that we were being asked to dance, and be joyful about it. One person's freedom became someone else's bondage.

The purpose in telling this little anecdote is to point out that there are a lot of things we do or expect in church, and that some of them have rationales lost in the mists of time. We've all heard homilies that

> *One person's* freedom
> *became someone else's* bondage.

bothered us; sometimes we live long enough to realise that they were built on a misreading of Scripture. For example, at 17, a lady caught me looking for "too long" in a mirror. She tut-tutted, "Vanity, all is vanity!" Fortunately, my Bible was NIV, where the verse was rendered, "Meaningless! Everything is meaningless!" (though the word *ephemeral* might be a closer concept). The idea of "earthly things are all in vain in the end" was a long way conceptually from Carly Simon's "You're So Vain."

Here's a curious thing. If I really had been a vain teen (and trust me, my complexion did not permit that!) and the Lord had wanted to pull me up for it, He could have used that comment to do it, incorrect though it was. He's thrifty like that, and not above getting His point across whichever way He can!

All that to say—it's worth it to examine some of the things we do, and recollect why we do them. It's good to go back to the source material and see if there really are grounds to go on doing things a certain way. If they hold up, they hold up. There are a lot of things we read into Scripture, and a lot of things we don't read at all—the Bible is *riddled* with puns, woven with poetry, and sprinkled with pop culture references that go over our heads because of linguistic and historical distance. It's a much richer document than we give it credit for.

I'm constantly coming across rediscovered information that sheds light on old texts, as Daniel 12:4 promised. Historian A.J. Froude said almost 200 years ago that moderns cannot hope to understand the mindset of England in the Middle Ages ... and here we are, daily trying to get our heads around first-century *Galilee!* While the writers' concepts are timeless, their expressions are coloured by their culture and their era and the style in which they laid those concepts out. The more we can find out about these colours, the better our understanding of what they were principally driving at. This is not revisionist. This is responsible. And we have the Holy Spirit to guide us into all truth. It's worrisome that we might be binding people to, or persecuting people over, traditions that never had a solid basis in the Bible in the first place. That's not to say God can't move through those traditions and mistranslations anyway—clearly, being thrifty, as I've said, He does. But it's a mistake, I think, to assume He moves *because of* such things when it might just be possible He moves *in spite of* them.

When we tell people, "Our church has the only correct interpretation, so don't go looking elsewhere," we are saying, "Don't trust." When we say, "Don't engage in negative conversation if you think differently," we are saying, "Don't talk." When we say, "It's sinful for you to feel unhappy or angry about this," we are saying "Don't feel." And these three things are known to psychologists as the three rules of dysfunctional families: "don't trust, don't talk, don't feel." Sometimes, there is even an element of "don't think."

We don't want to be dysfunctional. If there is nothing untoward behind the curtain of our Biblical interpretation, what is the harm in looking back there? There must be dialogue. There must not be a stranglehold on information. And there must be allowances made for people to feel what they feel. When we pray with the Psalmist, "May these words of my mouth and this meditation of my heart be pleasing in Your sight, Lord," we must choose our words wisely and kindly, and trust Him to continually move us along the path of sanctification. We must remember that there is a huge difference between a *fleeting thought* (which may not be our fault) and a *meditation* (which is a choice we make on where to place our focus). And even then, it's possible that Psalm 19:14 was merely David's postscript for the psalm he'd just finished—"hope you liked it, Lord"—and referred to it alone!

There are no Scriptural moratoria on feelings, as far as I can recall. King David bordered on bipolar in some of the songs he wrote. They often begin in the doldrums, kick themselves in the middle, and finish on a note of either hope or reliance on God. David's example shows us not that "people after God's own heart" have no strong negative feelings, but that they have the capacity to *redirect* those feelings once expressed and examined.

I find prayer meetings kind of strange at times. There's the one who does all the talking and doesn't leave anything left to be said by anyone else. There's the one who's so enthusiastic you feel rather lacklustre by comparison. There's the one who repeats the longhand title of God every few seconds. And there's me, kicking myself for noticing these things, giving myself a shake and trying to re-engage with God Himself.

What really doesn't help is when someone says something like, "Get up and walk around the room! You can't pray sitting down!" Granted, it's been a while since I've been told that. But how silly, to assume that everyone's method of focus is the same! Mine is to concentrate myself by curling up in a ball. It feels distilled, allowing me to give the Lord my undivided attention. If I have to get tactile with the world around me, my focus is divided. I am one part "with God," and one part with trying not to trip over chair legs, deciding where to walk next, and avoiding bumping into others.

As a singer and worship leader I was expected to be fairly physical onstage. You do it, and you make it into something sincere even if it doesn't come naturally, in the same way that you learn to incorporate playing your instrument with a certain amount of autopilot, so that it flows through you as you worship. However, you are still doing a multi-tasked job. You're still having to focus on more than just touching

> *The old have wisdom*
> *and the young have strength;*
> *but also the young have wisdom*
> *and the old have strength.*

God. It's even worse with walking in between rows of chairs; to me, it's immensely distracting. Ditto with trying to pray with deafening music on; I can't not-follow the lyrics, which precludes coming up with any words of my own, and produces mental and vocal incoherence. Others find deafening music an immersive experience that buoys them up to ride it like a wave. We're all different, and what works for one doesn't work for another. Therefore, it's counterproductive to make blanket statements about what "should" work for everyone. We'll just make half our people feel like aberrations. Focusing on Someone who isn't visible or audible can be hard work at times. It becomes much harder if you get the feeling you're not jumping high enough, or flapping hard enough, to make your leader feel like *they've* done a good job. Really, the leader just wants everyone to feel free to do business with God—but they should feel equally free to sit down, not clap, keep their eyes open and so forth, while they connect.

As I mentioned in the foreword, perhaps I'm reinventing the wheel. I just want to tackle things in a Berean way. There's no need to repeat the mistakes of the past, when I can go ahead and make new ones ... which is not to say that everything from the past is a "mistake". On the contrary. The past includes incredible moves of God, innovative in their time, and have left valuable legacies we lean on even today. The saying goes that "the old have wisdom and the young have strength". The reverse is also true. The old have the strengths of dependability and longevity on their side: it's why many love traditional churches and the sense of "home" they bring. And the young have the wisdom to chase hard after God, without heed to cost, however reckless it may seem, because He is God and He's got this and He may have new horizons for us.

Of course, not every entrenched leader has an entrenched mentality. Sometimes the trenches are the pews. Often the leader is a visionary, struggling to march us through the sucking mud that no one likes but no one knows how to get rid of. This is where vision-casting is so brilliant. If you can paint a picture of a desired future in God, and listen to input on that, and answer questions without feeling undermined, you may just get a groundswell of support. In our hurry to find new and better ways of doing things, don't assume that everyone in the room with longevity is therefore change-resistant. It's not universally true of the Old Guard even as it's not universally true of leaders.

I once heard a leader saying how great it was to get some new blood in the team. As a person who'd been taught *in that church* the wisdom of being "planted" (as opposed to skipping from one church to the next, avoiding accountability, stable growth and imperfect conditions), I found this a bit offensive. I started to wonder if perhaps the reason I wasn't getting anywhere was because I was considered "old blood" and they couldn't wait to be rid of me. Never assume that because someone's been around a while, they're set in their ways and can't dream. You don't know that. And you never want to punish faithfulness.

I don't mean to be confrontational, but if there are proposed system or method changes coming up in your church, ask the Lord to show you where the lines are between *true orthodoxy* and *your comfort zone*. While we serve the God of all comfort, His comfort is not limited to holding us close. Nehemiah, "God comforts," is also translated "the bread on the table." As we see in his story, often the comfort sounds more like, "You and Me, we've got this. Now get up and have at it." The Lord is our refuge and strong tower, and there we find not only a safe haven, but sustenance, and an armoury that equips us to get back on our feet and step out to face the future.

3 And What's Your Background...?

I'M A BIG FAN OF personality tests. I think they're useful tools for understanding people who are unlike ourselves. They help me make room for other people, to see them as valid even when I don't share their approach to things. Of course, I still secretly believe I'm right ... don't we all? And the same tests help me see that I'm not totally deformed, either, when I find myself unable to blithely adopt solutions that worked perfectly for the preacher. I can't take someone else's medication even for a similar ailment, and I can't see properly out of someone else's spectacles. It's not my script. They're likely to give me headaches into the bargain.

I guess there's a danger in too much categorising of others, though. By the time I nail down that I should be listened to as a valid viewpoint because of my age, gender, salvation status, denomination,

---

I can't take someone else's medication, *even for a* similar ailment.

---

generation, nationality, temperament type, Myers-Briggs designation, learning style, personality, church role, political leaning, spiritual gifts, love language, and because I'm not a natural blonde ... you can either conclude that these distinctions are so minute as to be meaningless as a tool for grouping anyone with any *other* one, or you can write me off as a ninny on the basis of just one of them.

The four temperaments:
choleric, sanguine, melancholy, phlegmatic

Many different kinds of people are born with leadership gifts, and many more develop them out of desire, push, or necessity. But there's no denying that there's a "leadership type". In America I believe they call it "Type A" (that would put me somewhere between "type LMNOP" and "type Z"). It's the temperament known as *choleric*, sometimes characterised as a tiger. People who are choleric-dominant tend to be movers and shakers, natural leaders, go-getters. They want everything done their way and done yesterday; they're big-picture people; they're always right. They can be bossy and domineering, but also doggedly faithful friends who believe in you and cheerfully give you the chivvying you occasionally need. They're more likely to hand you a cup of concrete than a cup of tea, but when it comes to being sold-out to Christ, they're second to none. They'll bat for you 'til Kingdom come, the whole time telling you there's only one place to buy really decent bats, and trying to pin you down to when you're going to go there. And these are the people most likely to seek leadership positions in, well, any organisation. And they're the people we love to hand those positions to, because, praise God, they always have a direction! and a plan! and they're always ready to launch it! They're positive, they love a challenge, they're competitive, they have forward momentum, and it's hard to keep up with them. They get things done in half the time as everyone else, because they don't bog themselves down with small details—they just get the job done. They're steam trains. They're impressive and dynamic and they inspire us. I get tired just watching them!

The next most likely candidate for a leadership job will be your *sanguine*. This is the happy-go-lucky, fun, popular, charismatic character. She's less like a president and more like a pop star or comedienne. She can occasionally generate a much more devoted following than even the president—right up until the moment everyone follows her over a cliff, because she was too busy playing on Facebook last night to remember to check the map! She only wants to be a leader while everyone is having a good time. She loves to start projects, but quickly gets bored with them and wants something new. She's disorganised, short on attention span, and can talk the hind leg off a donkey. But she's full of life and therefore magnetic; she adores people and makes them feel included on a grand adventure.

The *melancholy* leader is in danger of never implementing his plans, because he spends all his time fine-tuning them to death. They are an exquisite work of art. But he doesn't want to be a leader anyway, because he knows it will drive him nuts when people fail to sweat the small stuff the way he does, or even stick to the plan, or, heaven forfend, turn up. Things ought to always be done *properly*, if possible *perfectly*; and humans are altogether too *woolly* to perform like clockwork. Besides, you have to be in meetings all day, right? with … people. Who call you "pedantic" behind your back. So the melancholy sticks to his own corner, where he composes incredible symphonies and alphabetises his collected works of C.S. Lewis, and leaves the running of the place to people who don't find bringing one million random parameters into something cohesive *paralysingly intimidating*.

The amiable *phlegmatic* likes peace and quiet, with aeons of cave time, and church leadership is the very last place those things are available, unless you can pass off several successive days as sermon prep. So she smiles and nods and goes along with the bulk of it, heartily relieved that nobody has asked her to *run* anything. Flying under the radar is a way of life, but don't underestimate the value of the peaceful presence, the calm accepting smile, and the deep thinking that goes on under the still waters. Everybody loves, and loves to be around, the phlegmatic. They get nothing done, but they are rest personified. They help you un-knot yourself when you've overthought your Christianity.

It's easy to see from this short list that the bulk of the people who wind up in leadership are going to be people who are asking for it. And they'll tend to be, not exclusively but predominantly, choleric. So it's worth looking at our strengths and weaknesses and making an honest assessment of the job requirements and the skills we need to either have, harness or hire.

> It's worth looking at the skills we need to either have, harness or hire.

It's also worth nailing a plaque to the back of your mind that reads, "Other people don't have to be just like me." Because, you see ‹tongue in cheek›, we're right. Yeah, other people have *opinions;* but we're *right* ... right?

All of us are a blend of all four types, majoring in one or two. For every tabled decision, you'll have choleric members wanting to get on with the job (their way, of course); sanguine characters wanting to make it all a fun, social affair, organisation be hanged; melancholies enquiring about the research, strategy and implementation plans; and phlegmatics hoping the fuss will all blow over soon.

Let me have a flight of fancy for a minute. Let's envisage church leaders as the archetypes of their dominant temperament.

A choleric pastor can look out over her congregation and see people who need to have a bomb put under them to get them moving for Jesus and creating some kind of output.

A sanguine pastor can look out over his congregation and wonder why on earth these people don't have the joy of the Lord. What is *wrong* with them?

A melancholy pastor can look out over her congregation and see only the chaotic lives of people who refuse to follow the Nine Simple Steps to Godly Living.

A phlegmatic pastor can look out over his congregation and wonder why people get so het up about so many things when they could just chill in God.

BUT.

The Church is compared in the Bible to a body with many parts, all with their own function. No one part needs to feel inferior to another, or superior over another. And it takes all the parts to make the body whole—to make it the complete Body of Christ. So what if we, seeing all these different personality styles, stopped insisting that "becoming like Jesus" was a quest for homogeneity, and instead recognised in one another the many *facets* of Christ?

The choleric shows us the decisive aspect of Christ's nature. It's the part that stalks into the Temple to root out idolatry, usury and racism. It's the part who commands the wind and waves to be still, who bestows us with a new name and confers destiny. This is the God who finishes what He starts and marches inexorably toward the Cross.

The sanguine shows us the social and relational aspect of Jesus—spending time with people, hearing their stories, eating and living and laughing and crying with them, for God so loved the world that He came in person. This is the God who simply loves being with humans, and will do anything to achieve reconciliation.

The melancholy shows us the part of God's nature where we see how vital His Word is to Him, that not one full-stop is unimportant, that His great plan is detailed right down to the smallest component. They also manifest His deep pleasure in the beauty and intricacy of creation, that makes us behold the universe and exclaim, "How great Thou art!" in both senses of the term.

The phlegmatic shows us the compassion and acceptance of Him who said, "Come to Me, all who are weary and heavy-laden, and I will give you rest." This is the side of God which is patient and kind, longsuffering and faithful. This is the God who encountered broken outcasts and offered them a hope and a future.

We need all of these aspects of God incarnated in today's Body of Christ, since the original body was taken home to Heaven. I believe it may be part of what's involved in Communion: recognising around the table (or auditorium) the Body of Christ as it is here on earth today. And no single one of us can embody all of it. Growing up into the fullness of Christ is a group task, iron sharpening iron, fire in the Blood.

So.

Imagine if the choleric pastor sees, not laziness, but an army of people who have the skills to make her plan really fly, because they'll take care of all the small details, they'll make sure morale is high, and they'll keep everyone calm and looked after.

Imagine if the sanguine pastor sees, not depressives, but those who know how to mourn with those who mourn, those who know how to bring rest to the heavy-laden, and those who know how to research and problem-solve under pressure.

Imagine if the melancholy pastor sees, not mess and clumsiness, but people who can cut the Gordian Knot of thorny problems, people who can cheer up the sad ones, and people who won't judge her if she falls short in her pursuit of perfection.

Imagine if the phlegmatic pastor sees, not agitation, but people who can vision-cast, people who can spread the load of interaction and care for others, people who can get inside a simple idea and transform it into something magnificent.

Imagine.

If we were a team.

> *Imagine. If we were a team.*

Not a leader and bunch of followers. Not even a bunch of leaders and bigger bunch of followers. But a huge team. Where some people have a directional role, but all people have equal worth and input. A ... committee. From the word family of *commit*.

You may say I'm a dreamer, but that wouldn't be the half of it. How, you may ask, am I supposed to lead a team in a sensible solution, if we're all sitting around by the hundreds, talking endlessly about options that have already been eliminated and feathers that have already been smoothed?

The answer is, I don't know. I just want us to think about it. More in later chapters. For the present, I commend to you the Polder model my parents saw working well in the Netherlands church: everyone gets a say in decisions, even adherents with no formal membership. The eldership then weigh the input and make the decision with consensus, all parties feeling heard, even if not followed. If you do implement this method, you have to mean it. You can't just make your unilateral decision, and then make a show of consulting everyone so you can say you did.

I see a worrying trend in leadership discussions at the moment that hits one of my personal triggers. Because of this, take what I say next with a grain of salt: I may be projecting. But consider alongside that, the idea that if it hits one person's trigger, it may be hitting more.

Sometimes people talk about their leadership role in tones that radiate suspicion. They talk about how to manage people who don't "get" The Vision as though these people were the devil himself, and The Vision worthy of worship. It's like, "We're all up here, we're leaders, we get it, we're the good guys; everyone else—they're either sheep to be herded or trolls to be defeated. Give them half a chance and they'll destroy your vision, your reputation and your church." This negative, adversarial view of the laity helps no one. It doesn't help the laity, who can't work out why their pastor looks at them squinty-eyed and won't hear them out. It doesn't help the pastor, who has to live on hyper-alert and bear the whole burden alone, feeling persecuted and martyr-like.

A friend once said—tired of the grumbling during a rather difficult season in our church—that the best policy was to say to people, "There's the vision—and there's the door." But this "fit in or move on" approach is not pastoral at all. It ignores all the gifts and Spirit-leadings of the people the Spirit has sent to us. It puts The Vision on the throne. I've sat in on board meetings in the past. I know perfectly well that occasionally, vision, goals, and projections are things leadership *dig for* rather than *receive from God*. In the pew, I have no guarantee in a given season that the stated vision falls into the category of "God idea" rather than "good idea". Should such a variable then be put above human beings who are desperately trying to find their footing in an environment that seems oblivious to them? Have these teams forgotten that *ohana* means *nobody gets left behind?* Remember, it's not a corporation we're building. Nor are we a mechanised dairy factory producing homogenous milk. The Vision is not God. Just sayin'. The Branding is not God. Just sayin'. And speaking to both sides, being adversarial is the job of, well, the adversary. Also just sayin'.

In fairness, there is a massive amount of suspicion flowing the other way. People are always worried that a leader isn't telling them the full story, and often they don't stop to consider that maybe they really don't want to know the full story. Or maybe the full story violates someone else's privacy or dignity. And, let's face it, we're a nosy bunch. As we get older we realise either that we're nosy because we're bored, or that nosiness isn't serving us well now that we know what a let-down truth can sometimes be. To say nothing of how let-down we feel when we realise we've let ourselves down by stooping to it. If it was *my* multitude of sins (I speak here of *non-criminal* sins!) I'd sure want someone's love to be covering it from peering and jeering, while I was in repentance rehab.

It's a hard thing, to live in your freedom and yet to show forth plainly that you are above suspicion. But if you can, to the best of your ability and listening capacity, don't just *look like* you're above suspicion: actually *be* above suspicion. This should go without saying, but unfortunately it has to be said, because my lived experience and that of countless others tells me that this area doesn't get the attention it needs. Have integrity. Treat others with honour. Don't take liberties. Live what you preach. For that matter, project what you're preaching into others' lived experience—all four types of people—before you preach it.

Often, high leadership doesn't know there are grounds for suspicion in their middle management, until everything goes pear-shaped. This means the suspicion coming from the populace was justified all along. And it means the suspicion levelled at the populace wasn't. These are very, very difficult things, and if we were all perfect

What if we were on the same side?

people it wouldn't be an issue. We are all of us taking leaps of faith in each other every day.

What if we were able, by leap of faith, to lay aside suspicion all around, and we were on the same side?

What if questions were just questions, not challenges? What if they were asked out of a desire for clarity or reassurance, moving toward ownership of the idea, and not a deliberate attempt to be a stick-in-the-mud?

What if, instead of approaching your leadership role in terms of *Unwashed Them* and *Holy Us*—we remembered that in relation to the highness of God, we are all Them? And then imagine if we looked around at our fellow believers, leaders or laity, as though we were all Us? What if, to borrow from science fiction, we stopped perpetually saying nothing but "I am Groot!" and revealed our self-sacrificing side in order to enact a new truth known as "WE ARE Groot?"

Talk to God about whether there is a Great Divide to be bridged in your heart, even if the divide is not your doing. Ask Him for strategies for your team. "Because I said so" won't suffice, not any more. "Because we've always done it that way" is a tired non-answer. Division doesn't help us. There must be better ways forward, where you don't have to justify your vision and I don't have to feel like a naughty five-year-old. Let's see if we can find them together.

4 The Big Picture

YOU'RE FAMILIAR WITH THE PHRASE "the Big Picture"? It's a really, really useful tool for seeing the patterns and purposes of God. It's also a really, really inadequate way to plan methods of doing things that involve people.

Pastors who invoke the Big Picture are not wrong. The Bible itself is a Big Picture book (no pun intended, though many of us started getting interested in the Bible that way as children!). Having an overview of God's direction in history is hugely helpful. Having an overview of what He might be asking of a given church in a given season is also helpful. It's good to step out of the traffic and look at the road map: it brings reassurance and perspective. "We're here to win the lost, amen?"

The trouble with the Big Picture is that big pictures are always, always made up of small pictures. It doesn't matter if your church has

---

Big Pictures are always, always made up of small pictures.

30 dots per inch or 2400. How much resolution are you looking for? Your Big Picture is going to have to be enacted by everyone around you pulling their little pictures into alignment with it. And you need to remember that when people have issues with that, it doesn't always signify rebellion.

In computer graphics there is a thing called an *artefact*. A jpeg file (an image saved with a *.jpg* tag) is essentially a reconstituted recipe. In a perfect world, each time this file is opened and re-saved, it ought to perfectly recreate the recipe so the photo looks the same each time. But this doesn't quite happen. Over time, and multiple saves, the picture will acquire little glitchy patches of discolouration, errors called *artefacts*. This happens because the electricity supply does not always hit each given bit of the recipe at the exact same voltage each time. Again, in a perfect world, it would. But we aren't living in a perfect world, and consequently, jpeg files suffer these small data losses as time goes by.

Your Big Picture may have an iron-clad recipe, but you're not working with iron-clad pixels.

What this means in people terms is that while your Big Picture may have an iron-clad recipe, you're not working with iron-clad pixels. They're all subject to the whims of voltage variation. Some of your "pixels" are struggling in their marriage, or with anxiety disorders, or deep-rooted doubt, or strongholds of various kinds. Some of them are simply afraid of authority figures. Some of them are burned out. So, when you ask your people to be Big Picture people, you're asking them to lift their eyes, to operate in faith—and this is a good thing. But you must never lose sight of the fact that they still have to cope with operating in a Small Picture environment. And in that environment, it's easy for them to get damaged.

When the recipe doesn't go as planned, people get discoloured and discouraged, as well as finding themselves off-balance. We oughtn't victim-blame them for that by referring them to the Big Picture and asking "What the?" If you're going to do the "please explain", do it in such a way that implies not "why are you out of line?" but "I would love the chance to understand where you're coming from." Because we're not *just* here to win the lost. We're also here to be the family of God. And Jesus indicated clearly that the one (*that we have love for one another*) heavily influences the other (*revealing to the lost the One we are disciples of,* if I can put that construction on it).

> *We're not just here to win the lost.*
> *We're also here to be the family of God.*

I believe that, while inextricably linked, these two calls—winning the lost and being a family—are equally important in their own right. There's no adoption without a family to adopt *into,* so the question always arises: what kind of family is it? What's the dad like? What's the culture like? Does it encourage growth and development, a hope and a future? Will I be safe, and will you be there for me?

There's a temptation in living in the realm of the Big Picture. When you see the goal so clearly, you can become hyperopic: preoccupied with the future at the expense of the present. If *myopic* (in a metaphorical sense) is missing the wood for the trees, *hyperopic* is missing the trees for the wood, whilst several trees may actually be on fire, or be under attack from axes, or felled by earthquakes. You can be so heavenly-minded that you're no earthly use, though that's a rather harsh way to put it. The key to avoiding it is to *not look down on* those who are desperately grappling with measuring out their ingredients for the recipe, wondering where all the weevils have come from and why spoons are missing. It's about compassion, and identifying with others; and leaders have the difficult job of balancing their Big Picture with empathy for the Small Pictures, almost holding them in cognitive dissonance at times. It's a massive ask within a mammoth task.

There's also this: who says they are *small pictures?* What is the value of a single human soul? Is it really true that Jesus would have come and died for any single one of us even if we were the only one? Because if it's true, then no single one of us is discountable or expendable. If we build our churches ruthlessly at the cost of hurting and losing saints, then have we gained our collective world but lost our collective soul? I've seen incredible gifts bring many to salvation, but ride roughshod over many in the background, to the point where they left the church and, in some cases, the faith. This kind of revolving door is heartbreaking. It's not enough to *only* care about getting people saved—if all we're going to do with them once they're part of us is to neglect, abuse or take advantage of them. So if we bend over backwards for the unsaved, are they then fair game once they've said the sinner's prayer? Are the three incoming souls somehow more valuable than the three outgoing souls? Must we really gain by losing, and doesn't this misrepresent the picture we paint of "being added to daily"? Why must familiarity breed contempt, when we are supposed to show our lineage by our brotherly love? This isn't the picture of the Body we see in the Epistles. This Bride is shooting herself in the foot.

As an idealist, my heart aches when I think that we, the church, might be the only Jesus the world sees. Because despite centuries of our best efforts, we're terrible at it. And I don't know what the answer is. I want the world to see the perfection of Jesus, and I fear that all I'm showing them is how this particular rat deals with this particular trap and runs this particular race. Maybe that's all He's asking of me. Maybe, if the Bride was as perfect now as the divine Groom, we'd be horribly painful to deal with. Maybe it's the Bride's imperfections that highlight the perfections of the Groom. Yet ... don't we all long to be a credit to Him!

Jesus tells a story in Matthew 18/Luke 15. He asks, "If a man owns a hundred sheep, and one of them wanders away, will he not leave the ninety-nine on the hills and go to look for the one that wandered off?" He goes on to say, "In the same way there will be more rejoicing in Heaven over one sinner who repents than over ninety-nine righteous people who do not need to repent." It's worth noting that the sheep who wandered away and needed repentance (literally, *needed to do a U-turn*) was not a random unchurched person, but a person who belonged. You could make a case for whether or not Jesus was talking specifically about backsliders, or whether He saw *all* random people as "these are Mine and they belong"; but in the end, the ambiguity is beautiful, because it excludes no one. Outside sinner—inside sinner—one-foot-out-the-door sinner—all of us are worth dropping everything for, an all-out effort at restoration.

I find that incredibly encouraging. Because—despite the idea that a Truly Mature Christian™ will stoically suffer all the slings and arrows of outrageous leadership, in the name of getting the lost saved—few of us are that emotionally impervious. In fact, if we're going to extend the metaphor, the worst thing that happens to the group of "righteous sheep" is that they're briefly left unattended, trusting to their herd instinct to stick together and stay put. That would equate to, "You are not dumped for, or less valuable than, incoming or returning lost souls; you are simply allowing your leader to temporarily place his or her focus elsewhere, under emergency conditions." It doesn't mean the

The Big Picture

shepherd won't be back to return his focus to the flock's next meal. It doesn't mean the naughty sheep is being rewarded with all the attention. It means that the flock itself takes over the responsibility of ensuring that everybody present knows they're enfolded. And it means that the flock needs to join in the shepherd's concern that all other matters pale when one of us is hurting, and join in his or her joy when restoration occurs. But as I said, these are emergency conditions. The shepherd does not *routinely* leave the sheep eight hours a day to go recruit random strangers out on the hillside. That is not the pastoral function. The shepherd knows his or her sheep, and if one of them is missing, it causes concern.

The issue should not look like, "Who is, and is not, important in this scenario?" And the way to deal with the anxiety over the shepherd's preoccupation is to tell ourselves, "This does not mean the rest of us are not important; it merely means that right now—while one of us is in danger—we all need to be *less focussed on* our own importance."

---

*It does not mean
the rest of us are not important;
it merely means that we are
less focussed on our own importance.*

So is this search an exercise in hunting, or retrieval? If you consider the whole world to be *sheep from your fold* who have wandered away, you and your congregation might go nuts while you split your focus a million ways. Thus it's likely that the missing sheep represents a church member, not a non-member. The other two parallel parables—the lost coin and the lost son—underline this notion as well. They are things we have, that become lost—not things we don't yet have. And it doesn't matter if the ratio is 1:100, 1:10 or 1:2—when someone we love who belongs to our house goes missing, Jesus assumes we'll be obsessively looking for them. But sadly, what can happen is that the pastor shrugs and says, "I've still got 99. And I can't do anything about the one." Or even—and I kid you not—"Another one will come along." This person isn't thinking about the welfare of their sheep—only of keeping their numbers schmick. Fortunately, they are rare.

The other thing to consider is that when Jesus talks about Himself going to rescue lost sheep, He's got some excuse for pointing up the gap between their intelligence and His. A pastor, however, does not. He is just as human as his flock, though he may have an edge over them in spiritual training and wisdom. Jesus, while fully human, had a much, much bigger edge, with His direct line to the Father. I'm not sure if I should say that Jesus, at that point, had the Holy Spirit, because so do we all: I just don't like the idea of leaders with a Messiah complex looking down on those they lead as a bunch of dummies who don't know what's good for them. Maybe that's what we are. But maybe not. More on that shortly.

So, if it's not the pastor's job to go roaming the hills all day looking for sheep who might like to *join* the flock, whose job is it? Well, I'm glad you asked, and you know what's coming next, don't you? Having talked about the warnings of seeing *only* the Big Picture, let's go on and have a look at one of the truly great Big Picture ideas we find in Scripture.

In Ephesians 4 we get this wonderful list of job descriptions. It's prefaced by an introduction we sometimes overlook in our hurry to get down to brass tacks.

> *Be completely humble and gentle; be patient, bearing with one another in love. Make every effort to keep the unity of the Spirit through the bond of peace. There is one body* [and Hey! you are not the Head!] *and one Spirit, just as you were called to one hope*

when you were called; one Lord, one faith, one baptism; one God and Father of all, who is over all and through all and in all.

And here comes what we think of as the meat, though I think we just *read* the meat, myself.

So Christ Himself gave the apostles, the prophets, the evangelists, the pastors and teachers, to equip His people for works of service, so that the body of Christ may be built up until we all reach unity in the faith and in the knowledge of the Son of God and become mature, attaining to the whole measure of the fullness of Christ.

Then we will no longer be infants, tossed back and forth by the waves, and blown here and there by every wind of teaching and by the cunning and craftiness of people in their deceitful scheming. Instead, speaking the truth in love, we will grow to become in every respect the mature body of Him who is the head, that is, Christ. From Him the whole body, joined and held together by every supporting ligament, grows and builds itself up in love, as each part does its work.

All of this is further to Paul's previous conversation two chapters back, about placement and purpose, in which he says,

For we are God's handiwork, created in Christ Jesus to do good works, which God prepared in advance for us to do.

I'm not 100% convinced that these "good works" are individual good works, because the paragraph is full of plurals and collectives, which *could* indicate that these are group projects. But we can't discount individual works, either. It may well be another beautiful, intended ambiguity designed to free us up in both directions. It's certainly true that God deals with us as individuals as well as in groups, so individual works are not precluded, are they? So I'm going to proceed as though both things are true: that each of us and each church have a range of pre-planned activities in the will of God. It could be said that the fullness of Christ, the mature body, is always going to be involved in community engagement because that's where His drive is. (Yes, I know my personal Bible interpretation is rather elastic. No, I don't know what to do about it.)

Ephesians is such a neat letter. Look at all the wonderful, specific things in it. The Big Picture is breathtaking. It's idealistic and visionary. It shows us the shape of the thing we're to become. To summarise:-

- We are God's Stuff and we do God's Stuff
- God has specific Stuff planned for us to do, solo and/or in groups
- The Stuff is designed to help us all reach corporate maturity, be supported, know Christ, and attain to His fullness
- The results of the Stuff include corporate stability, discernment, loving truthfulness, and sustainability
- We operate from a place of humility, gentleness, patience, love, unity and peace *(four of these being Spirit-fruit flavours; one being similar; and unity being so important that it was reiterated seven times)*
- Skilled people are given to equip the church for the Stuff, and they are:
    - Apostles
      (sent ones, delegates, ambassadors, messengers, commissioners who operate the miraculous)
    - Prophets
      (foretellers, inspired speakers, poets—Strong's Concordance does not say 'forthtellers', though that may well be what it amounts to: pattern interpreters)

- Evangelists
  (preachers of the gospel)
- Pastors
  (shepherds)
- Teachers
  (instructors, doctors, teachers, masters). Paul didn't punctuate the same way we do, so these last two could possibly be meant as a joint "pastors/teachers" term.
- Some people are "ligaments" and their job is to maintain connections and hold everything together.

We are God's stuff and we do God's stuff.

So what's really curious about this list is that most of the Stuff appears to be *in-house*. Look at the purpose, and the results. Everything seems to be geared towards helping the Body grow up and grow well and grow Christlike. So if our SOLE focus is winning the lost, we are not being obedient to Scripture, any more than if we were ignoring the Great Commission in favour of perpetual redecorating. I am not saying God is limiting the Stuff to Interior Stuff; just that, *whatever* the Stuff turns out to be, it builds up the Body. This gives us some insight into the roles of apostle and evangelist, who don't need to keep *getting sent to* the found or *evangelising* the found, but whose work nonetheless *benefits* the found and largely *creates* the found.

You could make a case that the order is important. First God sends apostles—missionaries, if you like—to say, "Hey, there's a God and He has a plan." Then He sends prophets, to say, "Here's the general shape

The Big Picture

of things." Then He sends evangelists to say, "Here's the gospel, join us!" Then He sends pastors to care for the joiners and give them direction, and teachers to teach them, and finally various people to keep them in close connection to the rest. It's just a thought, and not a very coherent one, but there it is. I'm not trying to "bend" Scripture: I just love asking *what if*. Sometimes, let's face it, Occam's Razor (the belief that the simplest answer is the right one) is a rather blunt tool. I'm an amateur, but I like to play in the myriad levels of Scriptural interpretation and application. There's so much there.

Throughout this book I've used the word "pastor" loosely, as most of us do these days, to describe a person who leads a church. It is, in fact, a specific gift—one of five—with parameters and a focus. Applying the principles we used in temperament typing, let's see what happens when we type ministers by gifting, and stick them out there without diversified help.

A church run only by an apostle may seldom lay eyes on their leader. He'll always be off somewhere: that's his gift. When God says *Go*, he goes. He may possibly preach a lot of sermons focussed on getting people out into the missionfield. An apostle chained down permanently to a local congregation may go stir crazy.

A church run only by a prophet might have elements of unpredictability. This will keep people excited and on their toes, but won't make for a calm, stable environment. There could be a lot of sermons about listening carefully and hearing from God for yourself. Or, a lot of sermons claiming that since *he's* heard from God, that should be good enough for you! A prophet locked into purely local affairs will probably get bored and restless with a sense that he's called to bigger things.

A church run by an evangelist runs the risk of every sermon being an outline of the salvation plan, followed by a call to repentance. What's wrong with that, you ask? Nothing, except that it lacks any specific

The Big Picture

after-salvation instruction. It's like taking the *101* class over and over again and never getting to *102*. So this church's strength is that it gets enquirers saved; but doesn't know what to do with them next, and the risk is that the birds will come snatch up the seed. An evangelist forced to deal with the minutiae of your daily problems will probably tell you to take them to the Cross, and not have much else to say.

A church run only by a shepherd pastor could turn out to be a group who all feels loved and has some direction, acting in concert for the most part, but it will be unlikely to venture far from the sheep pen. It's got a good thing going (if very predictable), cozy and insulated. Sermons will frequently be about taking care of one another. This church will attract the broken who need to experience the love of Christ, but may lose members who want to translate that into some action which could rock the boat. This pastor may be flummoxed by people who thrive on—and generate—drama. She then has to work out how to administer discipline in such a way as to not take sides or lose the relationship altogether.

And a church run by a teacher may end up feeling more like a classroom than a family. You'll learn a lot from the teacher—more than you want to know, probably—but unless you're the studious type you'll soon dread Sundays and their monologues. The teacher knows everything, and can't wait for you to know, too—and there's always more. The unrelenting standards can mean that everyone is enrolled but nobody ever graduates. The teacher will feel frustrated as they observe that even though they told everyone *just last week* how to

---

Often non-people people wind up in these people-centred jobs.

deal with Issue X, people are still fussing about it and not using the strategies they were shown.

Personally, I like the pastor/teacher combination. But I'm not seeing it. What we see a lot of these days, is a church where there is one person at the top, labelled "pastor", being asked to do all five ministry gifts AND act as CEO, Managing Director and Financial Officer of a going concern. (Side note, not once in the New Testament is the church compared to a corporation.) Frequently, this person is not pastoral at all; he's typically an evangelist, great at getting people saved; or a teacher, great at expounding the Word; sometimes an apostle, great at church planting. Often this means that non-people-people wind up in these people-centred jobs.

It sometimes happens because we like to appoint brilliant leaders to the top of things, and brilliant leaders tend to be cholerics. Possibly, it's that cholerics are the ones rushing confidently to the front of the line when answering the call of God, and that's why so many end up in ministry. Cholerics are awesome when God calls, because they always see a challenge as a glass three-quarters full, and themselves as a tap. But unfortunately, they're not *primarily* relational. And a shepherd needs to be.

It might be a nice ideal to say that each leader should be all five things, as a hand should have five fingers; but I'm not convinced that the bulk of leaders can manage that, any more than they can contain four entire personalities. Certainly the most dynamic leaders tend to be specialists; it's their expertise in one given area that confers that charisma.

What a lot of churches do to mitigate the natural limitations of the person at the top, is to staff (or volunteer-fill) the gaps. This is very sensible. But I have yet to see a church website where the staff list is arranged and described according to ministry gift, i.e. "Apostle: Jane Jones. Prophet: John Citizen. Evangelist: Mike Drop," and so on. It would be awesome if every church fellowship had at least one person in each of the five categories, even if said person was out of town a lot. It would be useful if the head person of the church was described by their actual gift, rather than automatically and sometimes erroneously labelled "Senior Pastor". For one thing, though it may remind him or her daily of the need for pastoral kid gloves in their duties, it's going to sit like an accusation if that's not their gift, and the actual job is going to grind them down if that's the bulk of the work and they're ill-suited for it. It's fine if the head person isn't the pastoral one—provided *someone* is—but they should be honest about it. If you have a heart of gold but boots of lead, it's not accurate to market yourself as a golden goose.

It seems from the Ephesians passage that the fivefold ministry gifts have one collective job: to equip the saints. So it's worth looking at your leadership gifts and seeing how best you do that. You'll have a lot to offer—and if you know what that is, or at least where to start, so much the better. God will expand you and your portfolio as time goes by; take your pulse regularly.

> *The fivefold ministry gifts have* one *collective job: to equip the saints.*

What you don't want is to get side-tracked. Here I'm drifting into very tricky waters, and I'll try to be as careful as I can.

The call of God, both to individuals and to churches, is a very amorphous thing sometimes. Ever tried to sew yourself a garment, and been astonished at how hard it is to replicate the human form, which can be pushed, pulled, squeezed, bent, twisted, stretched and slumped into so many nonspecific curves? It's a bit like that. The shape of the human tripartite being is always in motion. We have design "rules" that we "except" from occasionally, as in the person who chooses to keep their temper even though they're normally volatile. God knows all the secrets of who we are now, and who we will be down the track: we do not. God knows what He wants to call you to now, to get you moving in a certain direction, but only He knows if it's the final destination or just ... a certain direction. For now. With a plot twist in the works! Add into that our human frailty—missed opportunities, bungled swipes at destiny, misunderstood instructions—and you just have to trust that whatever marks we miss, God will still lead us and anticipate us, often turning our failures into features along the way.

God will still lead us and anticipate us, often turning our failures into features.

So, while it seems clear to me from Ephesians 4 that the fivefold ministry gifts are for equipping the saints to do the largely internal work of growing up into Christ, that isn't to say He doesn't call people or churches to exterior work. That much is clear from other Scriptures and the example of those who lived in them. Maybe, Ephesians 2 is about exterior work and Ephesians 4 is the ministry to the interior. Then, we can have both; but I'm wondering if I've been unfair in expecting my pastors *et al* to equip me for the exterior works God has planned for me. I'm not sure if the Church is supposed to grow up quickly together into the fullness of Christ, and then take on Christ's exterior mission work; or if it literally takes until Kingdom Come for us to all grow up together into said fullness, and that is itself the mission. I'm leaning toward #1, but I'm doubtful it can happen all that quickly. Some limbs grow faster than others.

I find it baffling when a church is sharply one or the other, interior focussed or exterior focussed, choosing between maintaining and expanding. But then I'm passing judgment on someone else's servant, am I not? Even on God! I'm saying, "God shouldn't have called you to do *abc* and ignore *xyz*." And I have absolutely no right to say that. Because, just as it's an accurate metaphor that everyone in a given church is a "body part", it could be equally accurate to say that each local church is a "body part" of the worldwide "Body". And if that's the case, then *of course* some churches will major in one thing at the expense of another. But is the eye, brilliantly doing its seeing, really wrong for neglecting the vastly important job of hearing? So then what we're really asking is, how macroscopic should our outlook be? And now we're back at the Big Picture.

I just led you in a big circle, without solving anything. I just want us to *think* about things. If we have a church that's focussed on, say, its feeding program, will members feel known? Or if our church is focussed on, say, inner healing, will faith get around to producing works?

Every church has to decide where to put its focus, and that determines the face it shows the public.

Some churches are like the gym, existing for members but with open arms: "We have a lot of in-jokes and member privileges and some exercises that look really strange, because these are the things that keep our family healthy. Our focus is on thriving. So if you visit, you'll have to take us as we are and deal with the strangeness, but you just may get healthy yourself."

Others are more like a showroom, with the focus on marketing: "We're not crazy and we've got the decorum to prove it. We have a fantastic product that sells itself. Our focus is to display it in a lovely, non-threatening environment; so if you visit, we promise you will not encounter anything weird but you will still be shown the genuine article."

And, of course, a lot of churches are sleek reception areas, with a doctor's surgery tucked in behind them. "You can come and enjoy our coffee and nothing else; but if you need help, help is here. So if you visit, you won't necessarily see all of what we do up front, and you might leave, thinking we're shallow; but you might stay, be surprised at the depths hidden in plain sight, and be transformed."

So long as the surgery is well-equipped and staffed, it's up to the church how much they want to invest in the glamour of the foyer. The real question is, to what degree does a glamorous foyer really attract patients? Most pastors are itching to glove up and get into surgery. They genuinely care about transforming lives. But I wonder sometimes at the amount of money, manpower, stress and time that goes into maintaining a flash church. Don't get me wrong, I love experiencing it, even contributing to it. But is it *really* to impress the unsaved? A lot of unsaved people are far more impressed by the simple sincerity of the Christians they actually know. I wonder if some ministers are over a barrel. They want to do mission, but their congregations want a flash church to attend; and without the congregation, the pastor can't raise funds for the mission, so he has to agree to spending a huge amount on the means in order to allocate a little to the ends. Then people look at him and accuse him of being glamour-focussed, while all the time his heart has been burning for the mission!

The cart and the horse don't really have to be in competition, but they should be pointed in the right direction. The key is probably balance, and each church is going to draw the fulcrum in a different place, according to how they perceive their calling. If you're going to specialise in one thing, make room for the other things even if they're not top of your list.

The Big Picture

Every church leader must, at some point, ask themselves, "Am I equipping the saints? How, and what for? Or have I gotten side-tracked on some other project?" And then he or she will have to make a judgment call on whether the project, which may be very worthwhile, trumps the initial call of God to equip the saints around them, or whether both things are entwined together. Usually, such projects are directly about equipping the saints in some way—or about acquiring more saints. But occasionally they are not. That doesn't invalidate the project, but it might come into conflict with your leadership role, and you may end up having to choose between them. There are many incredible, God-initiated projects in the world (for example, World Vision). But it may be that a local church is not best placed to duplicate such projects. Especially, don't duplicate a ministry that *someone else* is already running in your town. Instead, think how gobsmacked they would be if your church supported *their* initiative! What brotherhood might be developed!

At some point, we have to define the function of the Church, as opposed to the many amazing functions of various parachurch organisations. And then we have to stick to it.

So what is the core business of the Church? To go into all the world and make disciples, baptising them and teaching them to obey all Jesus's commands to His own disciples. To be a family, a body, and a bride. To build the Kingdom and see His will be done.

Win the lost.
Be the family.
Build the Kingdom.

The Big Picture

Anything that lends itself to this picture is part of the call of the church. Anything extraneous is very cool and very worthy but not core business. This is known in business circles as *scope-creep:* when you set out to do a certain thing, and wind up doing a hundred extra things on the side because they've crept into the project. When it comes to side ministries, your church might be best-off planting it, outsourcing it, partnering with it, or sponsoring it—rather than making it central—if it looks like it might displace your *actual* core business.

Talk to the Lord. Ask Him what the core business is going to be for your fellowship—where it intersects with the master plan of winning the lost, being the family, and building the Kingdom. Ask Him where it fits into the picture that is even bigger than yours—your town, your country, your planet. Ask Him to help you hold the tension between the big pictures and the little pictures, or to bring alongside you one who can hold it for and with you.

5 Just Like JESUS Used to Make

THIS MIGHT BE THE MOST DAUNTING chapter of all for me to write. How *did* Jesus do leadership? The first instance we might call to mind is one of the very last in His earthly visit: washing the disciples' feet at the Last Supper. We note this as one of the pinnacles of servant leadership: the willingness to demean ourselves for those in our care, and to set the culture not just by words but by example. Jesus was probably subverting a whole bunch of Jewish norms when He wrapped that towel around His waist and got to work. When we look at Bible interpretations, we tend to think that the cultural norms of its setting are the norms we're called to adopt. But it might not necessarily be so. Jesus was, Himself, in His time, countercultural. Much of the Sermon on the Mount tells us that. "You want payback? Think again. You want to do the minimum? Think again. You want fair for fair? Think again. You think hiding sin in your heart rather than acting on it makes you pure? Think again."

Jesus had a big following, but His regular crew consisted of twelve men. They were a disparate bunch, blue-collar yet schooled in the Torah, political enemies, the wide-eyed and the sceptical, with varying personalities and agendas and tempers. They were real people, very real. Some of them had hoped for a rabbi to tell them earlier in life, "Come, follow me," and been told instead, "Go home, my son, and learn your father's trade." This was their second chance.

Disciples are often described by the phrase "ones who sit at the feet of a teacher". Interesting that it was Jesus Himself, at 12, who sat at the feet of the teachers. He was listening but He was also asking questions. Counsellors will tell you that it's the questions that guide the conversation. They were evidently returning the questions, because they were "amazed at His understanding and His answers." It almost sounds democratic, and I'm willing to bet that it was a rare thing for one so young to even be in conversation with the upper echelon, let alone to hold His own. The bar mitzvah had not yet been invented, and Jesus would have been a year shy of it anyway. Yet He sat at the feet of the rabbis before asking others to sit at His feet, even as He was baptised alongside those asking Him for baptism. Neither thing was particularly needful for Him personally—He already possessed both wisdom and purity—yet He did them anyway, perhaps in order to identify with us to the maximum extent possible.

What might such identification look like in our own ministries? I guess the starting point is to laugh with those who laugh, and mourn with those who mourn. At the more active end, *becoming all things to all men to win some* could involve taking up a trade to win the tradies, or in the case of some of the Chinese missionaries, going to prison to win the prisoners.

I don't know what the expected dynamic was between a run-of-the-mill rabbi and the disciples at his feet. Perhaps it depended on the rabbi. But for all I know, it could have been anything from an "I talk, you listen" scenario to a daily forum, or even a "just watch me and learn by osmosis" kind of a deal with no real interaction. I know that Jesus did it by telling parables, followed by Q&A. He was often bemused by the Qs and baffling in His As. He also took them on plenty of excursions, sometimes even sending them out without Him. It's as if He was a celebrity on tour and they were His entourage, but He actually mentored them as well as making use of them. When I say "making use of them" I don't mean in a mercenary sense. I mean that He let them participate and contribute. There's nothing like an object lesson to drive a point home. Picking up twelve basketfuls of leftovers from a five-bun picnic would be an experience that would stay with you forever.

In pedagogy there's a method teachers use called "I do, we do, you do." The teacher shows the students how to do an activity; then the teacher does it with the students; then the students do it alone. I think I can see this in the way Jesus operated. First He performed miracles. Then He had the disciples assist Him while He performed miracles. And finally He sent them out in teams into the countryside—and they came back reporting miracles.

Their salvation was much more important than anything they did as a result of it.

The goal probably wasn't simply to empower the disciples, though it did achieve that. There would have been multiple goals: bringing glory to the Father, demonstrating the delegated authority of Christ, foreshadowing the government of the future church, proclaiming the Kingdom of God, and bringing relief to the suffering. When they came back rejoicing, His comment was that the main thing wasn't their newfound authority but their identities being recorded in Heaven. He seemed to think their salvation was much more important than anything they did as a result of it. They may have been blessed to be a blessing, but they were also blessed because they were so dearly loved.

It's not an either/or dichotomy. Even in Abraham's story, where the saying comes from, it's not "I will bless you *to* be a blessing" but "I will bless you *and* you will be a blessing."

Even if we were to say that the rabbinical style of learning was a purely cultural thing—Jewish, First-Century—and that we needn't limit ourselves to that style of leadership, there's still much to be seen in the spirit, or Spirit, in which Jesus conducted Himself. That was characterised by inclusion, surmounting people's flaws and political leanings and pasts.

> *Jesus never asked anyone to do anything He wasn't prepared to do.*

It had elements of trust—that these demonstrably human people were being given a mission to reach the entire world. And He underlined all of it by never asking them to do anything He wasn't prepared to do— right up to going to the Cross and forgiving His crucifiers.

If you were to judge Jesus's leadership abilities by the quality of the people following Him, or the progress each was making in life, you could draw a number of conclusions, some incorrect. Some believers, like Mary Magdalene, had their lives turned around spectacularly. Yet Judas Iscariot lived in (or off!) Jesus's pocket for three years and never swapped out his own agenda for the will of God. Most of the disciples made much the same progress in that amount of time as we do; it takes a lifetime to conform to the image of Christ. I might like to imagine that if I'd been in His physical presence I would have gone forward in leaps and bounds, but it's probably not true. There were people all around Jesus all the time whose ears wouldn't take in the audible voice of God. We have another member of the Trinity with us 24/7 and we move at the speed we move at. The best we can do is listen, obey, and cooperate.

Oftentimes we tend to celebrate strength, success, progress, confidence and well-connectedness. Some of us look at ourselves and bemoan the fact that we aren't coming up to scratch. But this is not a Biblical outlook. Strength, success, et al are not bad things, but they're not the things Jesus talks about. What the Beatitudes actually call *blessed* is humility, sorrow, being misunderstood, the strain of "not being there yet" … perhaps because it puts us in a place of realisation of our need for Him. And the Beatitudes are, actually, a list of things He went through Himself. Nothing on that list which applies to you, is anything you need to be embarrassed about. It's glorious to hear about the turnaround in someone's life. And it's glorious to hear a person who is still waiting for their breakthrough say, "But you know what, God isn't finished with me. He won't let me go. He's walking with me, through all the messiness and craziness and mystery, and He's going to get me there in the end, even if I can't see that end yet. And I know *you're* walking with me too, and neither of you are going to give up on me!"

I'm sure in Jesus's larger following there were a wide variety of people in all states of disarray and at all levels of faith. We wouldn't judge Jesus's leadership on the state of the people following Him, would we? But we might be tempted to do that with each other. I've heard it said that the telling point of salvation is the condition of a person's soul. I'd rather point to the *direction* of a person's soul. You can be struggling as all-get-out, but if you're pointed toward Jesus, if you're following Him, if you're eyes are on Him—that's what matters. So while we could look at the rag-tag crowd that followed Jesus relentlessly from one place to another, and note that not many of them had haloes, that wouldn't mean that He wasn't a good leader. And if your congregation are similarly dishevelled, you needn't worry that it makes you look bad: it really means that you are attracting the people who need God-in-you the most.

And it's not a single sermon that most of them need, but a long-term commitment. In the same vein, if your following isn't huge, don't stress about that. It could mean that God has sent you a small number who need more intensive help, rather than a big bunch who don't need a lot. Jesus started with twelve, and they turned the world upside down.

Paul talks in 1 Corinthians 4:15 about the difference between "guardian" leadership and "father" leadership. He doesn't actually say very much, so we need to read between the lines to see what his point actually was. Here's what he said:

Even if you had ten thousand guardians [paidagogos] *in Christ, you do not have many fathers, for in Christ Jesus I became your father* [KJV: *I have begotten you*] *through the gospel.*

Because of the alternate translation of *begotten*, I think Paul is calling himself a *father* in terms equating to "I'm the one through whom you were born again." It may be an appeal to look back to the source: "I'm the one who brought you the gospel, you got it straight from the horse's mouth, which is a different matter from getting third-hand commentary from others." Or it may, indeed, be a warm, trusting parental relationship, if they had those then with their fathers, which I don't know. Your father is, in all times, a person you learn "lessons that stick" from. He's the horse's mouth, even when he's wrong.

Let's take a quick look in *Strong's* at this other word, *paidagogos*, from which we get our English word *pedagogue:*

"a boy-leader, i.e. a servant whose office it was to take the children to school; (by implication, (figuratively) a tutor ("paedagogue")):–instructor, schoolmaster."

I'm not sure if "boy-leader" means *a boy who leads* or *a leader of boys;* but in any case (bad pun warning!) he was *paid-a-gogo* to school with the master's kids. It's more like a supervisor role than that of an expositor, and he's a contractor, not a relative. I wonder if the church "guardians" Paul was referencing were people who preached, or people who simply stood by to assist anyone who hit a wall in their personal learning. I wonder if they were far less invested in the people, long-term, than Paul was. Then again, perhaps they were far more involved, functionally and relationally—as any parent would expect from a nanny delegated to look after their kids while they themselves are at work. But it's clear that Paul sees these roles as distinct from one another, 1:10,000. He's the father—he lays out the doctrine as he interprets it from God—and the others see that it gets taught.

> *If you are laying out the doctrine, also be prepared to be a loving parent.*

We're a long way forward in time from that particular horse's mouth. We still let the Bible's apostles set the overarching doctrines of the church, but we give massive weight as to how our leaders let that play out on the ground, with almost the same degree of deference. If you are prepared to lay out the doctrine for your church, then the other end of that stick is that you probably need to also be prepared to be a loving parent to them. And if you'd rather see yourself in the nanny role—chaplaincy, if you like—then your job may look more like coming alongside anyone who needs illumination, and paying close attention to their safety and wellbeing. Perhaps, all along, we've been talking about the difference between an *apostolic* role and a *pastoral* one. I've never really considered the apostolic call in terms of relational parenthood. We use the phrase "the church fathers" synonymously with either "church planters" or "Council of Nicea", but it's a *distant* descriptor, not at all an intimate one. The "church fathers" are people up on a pedestal somewhere, or carved into cathedrals—not people who will stay up all night with you, hammering things out.

There's an outside chance that Paul was being sarcastic (as we know he liked to be!) when he said "I became your father." He may, just possibly, have been snidely referencing Jesus's commandment, "Do not call anyone on earth 'father', for you have one Father, and He is in Heaven." (Matthew 23:9) If that should be the case, then the passage would have the sense of, "Guess how many Fathers you're meant to have? You adopted me as your dad, when you should have been adopting God alone. I'm just one of ten thousand teachers. All I do is walk you to school; next to Him, I'm nobody."

It's hard, isn't it, to judge how far metaphors ought to be taken! No analogy is so perfect that it can be extrapolated out to the nth degree. We glean what we can, and hope we've got it right. The Bible regularly mixes and intertwines and enmeshes metaphors because there just isn't one good metaphor that is big enough to encompass the whole salvation story. In the end, there's nothing like it; we can only find small similes with which to unwrap it one bite-size piece at a time.

Try this analogy on for size: a church leader (putting aside the dual role as a member of the Bride of Christ) is rather like the Best Man for the wedding of the Lamb. He's got a special role with a set of responsibilities. He dresses snappily in his Tuxedo of Righteousness, but he's not a patch on the Groom who gave it to him. His goal isn't to upstage the Groom anyway, but to show Him off, and to render all due assistance. He's one of the Groom's most trusted friends, and knows his appointment is a high honour and a humbling privilege. He's perfectly happy for the Groom to delegate some jobs to his fellow groomsmen,

The Bride belongs to the Bridegroom.

because they're all in this together with the same goal: to facilitate the union of the Bride and Groom. It's a collaboration, never a competition.

The Best Man may care deeply about the Bride, but he knows she doesn't belong to him. He respects the Bride as the Groom's wife. The support he gives her is not to woo her away, but to move her closer to the Groom. We see a good illustration of this in the attitude of John the Baptist: "I had one job. I told you straight up I'm not the Messiah—just His delegate. The Bride belongs to the Bridegroom. The Best Man is on call, and stoked when the call comes. And I am! Job done. He takes centre stage; I'll be in the wings." (John 3:27–30, paraphrased)

The Best Man knows wonderful things about the Groom that the Bride doesn't yet know. He gets to tell her, thoroughly and enthusiastically, all he can in his promotion of the Groom. He tells the truth, the whole truth, and nothing but the truth. If the Bride gets sidetracked, it won't be through any doing of the Best Man's! And he is super-careful every time he has to drive the Bride anywhere. The Groom won't thank him if she gets injured in a crash.

All of this sounds very full-on. Let's balance it with one of most beautiful things Jesus ever said, this passage in Matthew 11. He basically spent most of the chapter observing that haters gonna hate. Then He switches to praying to the Father, followed immediately (perhaps this is how He "does what He sees the Father doing") by these incredible words in Matthew 11:28:

Come to Me, all you who are weary and burdened, and I will give you rest. Take My yoke upon you and learn from Me, for I am gentle and humble in heart, and you will find rest for your souls. For My yoke is easy and My burden is light.

I always thought that when Jesus said "take My yoke upon you" that it meant He had some custom-built thing to lay on me. Custom-built for *Him*, that is: His own yoke, descending upon me, lowered on a string from on high. But if the phrase "do not be unequally yoked" has any meaning, then oxen were probably yoked in pairs. So to take on *Jesus's* yoke (the one He's got on) and learn from Him, would be to actually partner with Him, to slip in next to Him and be harnessed to Him, to let Him show me the ropes first-hand: not from a lofty height, but from right beside me in the harness. He's not offering to crack the whip; He's offering to hold my hand. Whatever the load is, we shoulder it together. And He promises that it will fit us just fine, and result in rest, not striving. How can work be rest? And yet that's the promise.

If your people are finding their yoke uneasy and their burden heavy, if they're stressed out living up to the expectations of their role, permit them to examine whether or not they're in the right yoke: next to Jesus. Examine whether the yoke you're encouraging them to wear is right for them. Build them one that is. Look at all the yokes in your staffing requirements and make sure all of them are rest-work. This is what you're looking for—Matthew 11:28 in *The Message* version:

To take on Jesus's yoke is to slip into harness next to Him.

Just Like Jesus Used to Make

> *Are you tired? Worn out? Burned out on religion? Come to Me. Get away with Me and you'll recover your life. I'll show you how to take a real rest. Walk with Me and work with Me—watch how I do it. Learn the unforced rhythms of grace. I won't lay anything heavy or ill-fitting on you. Keep company with Me and you'll learn to live freely and lightly.*

Mel Lawrenz writes,

> In Christian ministry people are not a means to an end, they are the end. This is fundamental to the idea of human dignity. People on the staff of a church should feel as though, at the end of the week, something was added to their humanity, not taken away.

People are not a means to an end, they are the end. — Mel Lawrenz

---

People do sometimes get "pruned", but let's look at that, too. Paul Ellis, through Bruce Wilkinson, has some insight into the mysterious comment Jesus makes in John 15:1–2:

> *I am the true vine, and My Father is the gardener. He cuts off every branch in Me that bears no fruit, while every branch that does bear fruit He prunes [or cleans] so that it will be even more fruitful.*

He notes that "cuts off" *(airo)* is a poor English translation that is rendered more often elsewhere in the Bible as "takes up" or "lifts".

Vinedressers don't take away the unfruitful branches that are withering in the shade; they lift them back up into the sunlight so they can fruit again. God isn't ruthless or mercenary, interested only in our production rate. We aren't commodities. He isn't paring us down, He's building us up. And we don't need to cut off our troubled people from ministry opportunities, but to lift them up. Sometimes all they need is a little light and warmth.

God isn't interested only in our production rate.
He has an Individual Education Plan for each of us.

God deals in the Big Picture and the small pictures. It might be unorthodox, but I believe God has an Individual Education Plan for each of us. He told us to work out our own salvation with fear and trembling (not the salvation of our neighbour). The general shape of appropriating the gift of salvation never changes—it still has to pass through the bottleneck of faith in Jesus—but the way He brings us to drink those living waters varies incredibly. And the way He coaches us, fitting us with the exact yoke that will bring out the best in us, is infinitesimally individual. So when that poor adulterous woman is thrown down at Jesus's feet, He makes a choice about how He's going to handle it. He can stone her, according to the old plan, or He can write her a new plan. It is her wrong to right, but His right to write. He bends down into the elder dust from which He formed her—not the latter stone of Law and judgment—and He begins to write her a new destiny, in the authority He had before the world began.

I have a lot of unanswered questions about what's in my IEP and the frightening things I see in others' journeys. I can't tell you why some people get abused and some don't, some people get healed and some don't, some are martyred and some aren't. Hebrews is clear that both sets of people are people of faith. I can only tell you that God has been faithful to *me*, and I expect Him to continue to be faithful. And I can tell you that He's not just interested in how productive I am: in fact at times He has *ensured* I cannot be productive, in order to show me how His flourishing love remains with me despite that. God describes Himself as a refiner of silver—one who unswervingly watches, guiding developments minutely—and a potter—one who uses a light and uninterrupted touch to create things both functional and beautiful. Since God cares so much about how I'm developing as a person, appeals to get out of my own head and work the Big Picture have limited mileage with me. They can be equally inspiring or discouraging. I'm never going to cease being a real person, even while focussed on the lofty.

> *Some get their miracles and some don't ...*
> *both sets of people are people of faith.*

Physiotherapists will tell you that the human body experiences pain in a rather roundabout fashion, via the brain. The brain, if faced with multiple crises, will automatically sort them by priority. This is why a man with a broken leg can run on it out of a burning building, and not feel the break until later. His brain has prioritised "save my life" above "fix my leg".

If we apply this to the Big vs Little Pictures, it means that there will be times when we need to suck it up and put the church vision first.

But it does not mean that the broken parts of us can be left unattended forever. They are allowed to matter too. We ought not to lurch from crisis to crisis, dragging our wounded. Far better to plan things well from the get-go, so that make-or-break crises don't arise so frequently, and good ongoing care can be given to all.

Try your best not to make people feel that if they are in pain, it is because they are insufficiently dedicated, or otherwise deficient. If your definition of *maturity* is *unemotional robot,* consider why we were created with freewill and emotions in the first place. The fact that I *can feel* tells you something about the God in whose image I'm created. He Himself is never at the whim of His emotions; mine, however, burst out like streamer poppers. I can control how I display that emotion, but I can't help its arrival. There will be times when I'm annoyed, bewildered, stressed, and down.

James 1 talks about operating from a place of maturity. I don't believe he is talking about *perfection.* I'm a big fan of renovation shows, and I find it a useful analogy for personal maturity. Immaturity is like a fixer-upper apartment where the walls are falling in and what's left of the carpet smells. Maturity is an apartment where all the structure is complete, compliant, and in place; it's painted, furnished and ready to move into. And perfection is when it's been fully staged by a master stylist with quirky art, lush textiles and beautiful things. In our immature state, the best we can offer others is shelter from the storm. In maturity, however, we make a warm sanctuary, conducive to further growth and healthy living. And as we edge toward perfection, we are changed from glory to glory.

Talk to Jesus. Let Him remind you that He is no quitter. He will finish your story and lead your faith to its fulfilment. Let Him show you that He, too, is an emotive being; that while He is never out of balance, it is not a question of Him having *no* emotions or *different* emotions, but of having *richer* emotions and in far more dimensions than ours.

> God's emotions are not so much
> other, *as* richer.

Ask Him to manifest His fruit in you. Ask Him for the best ways to manage people, with all their quirks and demands and multifaceted journeys.

For myself, I'm not sure I *can* live permanently on a mountaintop, where I always feel great and give 110% all the time. But I can turn my face to the light, and wait for each emotional storm to pass, throwing up a Scriptural umbrella now and then in the waiting. You can stand under it with me, if you like.

6 One Plus One Equals Three

LEADERSHIP, BY DEFINITION, IS A community activity. It's influencing the attitudes and behaviour of others, by acting not as a forklift for moving them in a desired direction, but as a magnet pulling them along with us as we forge on ahead. Good leadership should encompass the welfare of the followers and team, as well as the attainment of goals.

Leadership in the Kingdom is servanthood, as we all know. C.S. Lewis warns one of his fictional princes in *The Horse and His Boy*,

> "For this is what it means to be a king: to be first in every desperate attack and last in every desperate retreat, and when there's hunger in the land (as must be now and then in bad years) to wear finer clothes and laugh louder over a scantier meal than any man in your land."

Leading others is no glamour role, but the hardest and often the dirtiest job. In addition there is the weight of responsibility, the sting of constant criticism, and often fatigue as well.

Good leaders, while understanding the chain of command, aren't hung up on it. They of course are subordinate to God themselves, if not to an earthly upline as well. Christine Caine says that the best leaders are good followers. They ought to work towards being responsive (not reactionary) and decisive in the final analysis. They need true friends. Steve Taylor, a noted singer/producer and youth pastor, remarked that he values closeness with people who "are very unimpressed with Steve Taylor!" Accountability keeps a leader in touch with realism—and their own humanity. In this way they are consistently able to sympathise with the weaknesses of others, as Jesus identified with us. In the same way, a leader, though ahead, must never be aloof. He or she must use their skills to take people onwards, and also use their humanity to remain relevant to those being led.

The trait I personally most admire in a leader, after *kindness*, is *personal growth*. When I hear a leader say, "I used to think *abc*, but now I believe *xyz*," I rejoice. It shows me that this is a leader who is still reaching and growing. It doesn't make me feel iffy about listening to them. Instead it reveals a level of humility—a willingness to admit they weren't perfect—and a commitment to keep learning rather than to plateau out, having "arrived". Paul, at the end of his life, was still calling for his parchments, because he knew that there were still fresh things to discover and write about God. And if he was going to go out, he was going to go out searching the heart of God.

We will never run out of fresh things to discover in the heart of God.

I think that there are a lot of leaders who perform their job description but don't *express* their love and concern for those "under" them—giving the impression that they just don't care. This is rarely the case! A lot of misunderstanding could be avoided if leaders began with the premise (or better yet, a declaration) of love, and went from there. There are some who have no leadership titles, but who nevertheless have great influence on those around them, simply by virtue of the love and nature of Christ being manifest in their lives.

Let's have a closer look at the community aspects of church life.

"If two of you on earth agree about anything they ask for, it will be done for them by My Father in heaven. For where two or three gather in My name," Jesus said, "there am I with them." (Matthew 18:19–20)

This was a conversation Jesus had with His disciples in the general course of things. It's an interesting passage because it's one of only two times He was recorded using the term "church" *(ekklesia)*. He talks about having two or three witnesses, both for conflict resolution and for making requests of God. I've wondered why He specified that He would be present when they were in a group, when in John He seems to indicate that He will be within each one of us anyhow. Perhaps it's about the checks and balances built into corporate prayer: you can't ask God for a Ferrari in a prayer meeting without someone disagreeing with you! He could even be implying that if you're going to ask God for things, don't do it alone. When He says in several places that He or the Father will do whatever the disciples ask, He's always speaking to them as a group. It could also be about corporate faith carrying more weight.

We've talked a lot about being the Body. There's so much there, in regard to unity and diversity. I always find sermons on unity daunting. It hits my Worry Button. I know this is irrational, but in the interests of helping you understand the quirks of some lay people, let me show you how this button works.

When people ask for unity in the congregation—"We're doing such-and-such, and we want unity on this issue!"—I get frightened that they are asking for mass blind allegiance. How do I know that they've researched the issue? In my head, I see rows of uniformed Nazis, saluting, and despite my need to belong, I want to run screaming from the room. I feel like I'll be asked to lay down my individuality, my brain, and my calling for someone else's cause—a cause that often isn't one I'd have picked (which is neither here nor there, since I'm not the boss, but if you're going to lay yourself down on an altar, you kind of want to choose which one.)

> *When we use the term* unified, *do we really mean* homogenous?

I fear that when we use the term *unified* often we really mean *homogenous.* This is probably just a personal fear, born of having to "take one for the team" a few too many times. And it hits all my You-Do-Not-Fit-In fears. Suddenly I see a stadium filled with Maroons fans, and me sitting in the middle of them, and I've accidentally worn light blue, and I don't own a Maroons shirt, I had no money that day and they didn't have my size and I don't wear maroon well, and I'm unable to blend in, and I'm feeling the weight of my poverty, and then feeling indignant across the shame, because I'm still a person.

I'm the one who's responsible for outwitting these idiotic overreactions. I don't have to pay attention to them; I can refocus. I can use one of the Scriptural metaphors to do it, providing I can be assured somewhat that my church is doing it back. So I can remind myself that we don't all have to be copies of the one body part—in fact the whole project would fall over if we were. And if my church demonstrates that diversity (as opposed to *ad*versity) is welcome, so much the better. I can try to see us as a band, even: all playing different instruments, all playing different harmonies, but contributing to the same symphony, with nothing jarring. A song can be hummed by a single person, but that's nothing compared to when everyone plays their part, layering the melodies and countermelodies and the percussion and the highlights and dynamics ... that takes an orchestra, where even one missing instrument diminishes the whole.

What I'm about to say might sound a little Miriam-ish: "Is Moses the only one God talks to?" But let me assure you, that's not my intent. I am not rebelling against a specific authority in my own life—let alone when a nation's survival is at stake—nor yet operating within a dispensation where the Holy Spirit carries individuals along temporarily, rather than indwelling every believer permanently. What the church has been given in this epoch is astounding. Even to see Him through a glass darkly is a miracle that widely outstrips hearing everything secondhand.

It seems unlikely that God would give us a pool of saints, all of them bearing spiritual, motivational and natural gifts, only to have us restrict ourselves to using the gifts of the people in the board room. At times it has seemed like only one person was permitted to prophesy, the unspoken rule being, "If God's going to speak to this people, He's going to do it through ME." At other times it's seemed like the only ideas a church will endorse are ones that are generated at the top. When this happens, it's an enormous pity on the humanity scale, and an enormous waste of resources on the strategic. If we take the attitude that *we're not here to further people's ministries,* how do we answer Ephesians 4? That is *exactly* what church leadership is there to do: to equip the saints to do good works. If God has prepared such works in advance for the general folk in our church to do—and I'm speaking of stable people, not the spiritual lunatic fringe—are we really willing to tell Him

He was mistaken? Are we sure we want to hamstring the plans of the Father in other people's lives? Would you do that to your own kids? We are supposed to be family, aren't we? If a person is denied altogether a chance in their church to pursue the works God's planned for them, must they choose between obeying God and obeying His deputies?

I'm a little sorry to even use the term "lunatic fringe". God has plans even for those of us who are damaged and wild-eyed, cagey and crusty, young and impetuous, or fallen as far as you can fall. Leaders, of course, have to carefully balance the level of the left-fielded-ness against the benefits of letting the left-fielder know their contribution is significant, and the unknowns of letting the left-fielder loose on everyone else. You just don't know whether or not they are going to be a blessing or a catastrophe, and most churches won't take that risk, either because they wish to protect their people or because they wish to avoid a spectacle.

I know of one "gym style, spectacle friendly" church where everybody can play a part, regardless of whether they are homeless, mentally ill, or recently released. Their rule of thumb is "you can be as bizarre as you like, as long as you are never abusive." *Abusive* is outlined clearly and privately to the scarier members, as are any necessary limitations (especially regarding children). This church is a beacon of hope and inclusion for the misfits Jesus came to save. We might not be brave enough for full inclusion of the different, but we must be careful not to develop a caste system, with the Elites at the top and the Untouchables at the bottom. From the mouths of infants

---

We must be careful not to develop a caste system.

God has ordained praise, and we shouldn't discount "unlikely" people, thinking they have no blessing or word from God that could benefit us. If God can speak through a donkey, He can surely speak through any human surrendered to Him. If the Holy Spirit is in each of us, to guide us into all truth, then it's even possible for unordained people to have as much validity as the pastor. At the very, very least, learning to show kindness and respect to people we find difficult ought to help ripen the fruit of the Spirit in us.

Surely the best way to tell if a left-of-centre person is able to minister responsibly, is to be in real relationship with them. Obviously, the larger the church, the less likely it is that the person at the top is going to have solid relationships with every single person in the church. That's what a team is for. George Barna's research in the 90s reported that one leader can effectively minister to the felt needs of 8–9 people. I'm not sure if that includes their own family members or not. More recent statistics say that a fellowship group peaks at 20–30 people, depending on culture. Either way, there should be someone watching over you and out for you whose focus is not divided more than 30 ways, and preferably not more than 9. This realistically allows for people in a church to be known and supported, at the approximate ratio of a teacher to a classroom. If you ask a teacher about any one of their students, they will know that kid and their story quite well.

Psalm 139 is often given to people who are struggling with significance. I believe it also contains an ideal structure for counselling. Too often, leaders are asked to give advice to members who have barely given the leader a chance to know them. It can be like going to a strange doctor, telling him none of your medical history or current prescriptions, and asking for medication. But look how it works between David and the Lord. I believe there's something in following the sequence in verses 23 & 24, rather than skipping directly to the end as we often do:

1. *Search me:*
Ask me the right—Holy Spirit-led—questions. Then,

2. *Know my heart:*
Listen to me; try to grasp the motives and worldview I'm operating from, without prejudice. Then,

3. *Test me:*
Verbally run scenarios past me and ask, non-combatively, how I would approach them. There could be a gap between my motives and my methods that I'm not seeing. Then,

4. *Know my anxious thoughts:*
Even when they're unfounded, they shape me and the way that I interact with others and with systems. Only then:

5. *See if there is any offensive way in me:*
Is there anything you can show me that I might correct, that could be blocking me from moving forward? Are other people's claims about me founded or unfounded? Am I beyond the pale? ... And only now are you truly in a position to:

6. *Lead me in the way everlasting:*
Walk with me, individual to individual. Don't just tell me I'm sick—rehabilitate me. Don't just run me through whatever generic mechanism is in place—pray with me that God might continue to guide me in the IEP He has for me. Look at my IEP, if you can, and work with it.

The cure for heartache used to be to "count your blessings, get your eyes off yourself, and go do something for someone else."

Unfortunately, that just sends the pain underground to fester. It's like having a dead possum in your roof. You know something stinks, but you're not sure what or whereabouts it is, and you've been told to stop moping and go vacuum next door. It denies you permission to either grieve or heal, invalidating your personhood.

Sooner or later, wounds have to be properly examined and dressed. Sometimes they are too profound for a pastor to handle alone. Psychology and pastoral counselling both have their limits, but together can encompass the problem from both ends. Trained inner healing prayer ministers can be an enormous help. Network where you can, knowing that we all want the same thing: health for our people, no matter who it comes through. Try to see psychology in the same light as medicine. It doesn't cure all, but it cures much, and to some degree it cures what you can't, if miracles aren't happening. God isn't always forthcoming with either psychological or physical instant miracles. I can only assume it has to do with the person's IEP, that perhaps the longer road, or the reverse order, or the involvment of others, has benefits none of us can fathom.

Big churches are awesome, and they can be even more awesome if their policies have elbow room in which tailored solutions can be sought and applied. I don't know how this can be done without the appearance of favouritism, or inconsistency. But I do know that love seeks to restore, and bends where it can. It has to be more than a structure. And you can't parent unidentical children identically, anyway.

I love large services. I think they're magical. In my 20s I loved to lose myself in the solidarity, and soar on the noise, soaking in the presence of those around me as well as in God's. No doubt some enjoy the anonymity a big church offers—the ability to slip in and out on days you can't face small talk. It's a good place to heal when being left in peace in God's presence is what you need in that season. The pressure is much less. Given a little time to catch your breath, you can then start to interact more and start giving back. The other great thing about a big church is that it can take on, or fund, big projects, or a big portfolio of smaller projects. It has clout.

The older I've got, though, the more I love small church. It's intimate, but there's still room to breathe. It can have just as many mystical moments. I love it when the music falls and the hairs on the back of your neck stand up and you know God is speaking. And in a corporate sense, your contribution and your absence make a much larger difference. You've got a fighting chance of being known and trusted and missed. If the pastor calls and says he notices I haven't been around, he's not saying, "My numbers were down—where were you?!" He's saying, "Is everything okay, can we help with anything?" I attend a small congregation that's a subset of a larger church, and I also belong to a fortnightly "life group" of about 12 people, so I've got the best of all three worlds. Life group is vital to me; it's home, where I can be real, warts and all. We eat and learn and pray together. We don't always agree—it's anything but an echo chamber—but we try to give each other grace, and it never descends into a slanging match. The leader facilitates, soothes and smooths with wisdom, without ever raising her voice. It's not at all mystical: we support each other on the ground. Here's my theory: magical, transformational moments happen in church, but growth and discipleship happen in life group. Revelation happens in both.

The New Testament churches probably varied in size, but some of them were meeting in homes. I don't know if the apostles patterned

---

Transformational moments happen in church, but growth and discipleship happen in life group.

their new assemblies roughly after the runsheet of their former synagogues, for lack of other ideas, or if it really was some inspired new thing. Synagogues themselves are not mandated anywhere in the Law. Even the Tabernacle and Solomon's Temple did not seem to require twice-on-Sabbath meetings with three fast songs, three slow songs, Communion, offering, announcements, a sermon and an altar call. It makes you wonder how we ended up with formally structured services to begin with, and why we insist that propagating them is the only way to plant and run a church. Paul gives us a fairly loose outline across three letters of how he sees our gatherings running:

When you come together, each of you has a hymn, or a word of instruction, a revelation, a tongue or an interpretation. Everything must be done so that the church may be built up. (1 Corinthians 14:26)

Be filled with the Spirit, speaking to one another with psalms, hymns, and songs from the Spirit. Sing and make music from your heart to the Lord, always giving thanks to God the Father for everything, in the name of our Lord Jesus Christ. (Ephesians 5:18–19)

Let the message of Christ dwell among you richly as you teach and admonish one another with all wisdom through psalms, hymns, and songs from the Spirit, singing to God with gratitude in your hearts. (Colossians 3:16)

While "everything must be done," it doesn't have to be done *all on the same day*—provided that in the course of things, everything does eventually take place. You and I both know of churches who have never been keen on facilitating "a tongue or an interpretation," yet

Each *of you* ...

have completely enshrined "a hymn and a word of instruction." This will be news for them: not everyone thinks that communal singing is a great experience that leads them into the presence of God. I do—but I'm a singer and songleader, daughter of a singer and a songleader, so of course I love it! Yet we must address this idea that *worship = singing*. It is not necessarily so—but that's another book. Suffice it to say that while many modern people delight in roaring ditties at football matches, concerts and karaoke nights, many others find mandatory corporate singing uncomfortable and unnatural. And so this, far from ushering them into communion with God, can become an extra obstacle to communion with God, as we noted in Chapter 2 with the dancing.

The thing that leaps out at me is the level of participation. *Each of you. Speaking to one another. Teach and admonish one another.* This is not *Let the pastor do it.* This is *Everyone do it.* And these are things you can't really do in a large meeting. When was the last time we tried *each of you* in an auditorium? We could conclude that meetings were never supposed to be large; but we could equally say that Paul (who was only human) didn't anticipate how huge a church *could* grow, and so didn't leave contingency instructions for that. But you *can* do *each of you* in a life group.

In a life group, everyone's got something to contribute: a beautiful song they found on YouTube, a neat quote they read in a book, something God showed them in prayer, a specific message in tongues (there's no reason this can't come to the sharer days in advance) and a person who can interpret it. I suppose if your life group is a sports-based one, you can't do these things while engaged in actually playing football. And then we're back to *what kind of group is it,* just as we asked *what kind of church is it*—outreach or inreach, gym, showroom or clinic? Both outward community care and inward community nurture need to happen at some point, whether via big church or small church or teeny tiny home fellowship—or the Good Thing you've got going is not a church at all, but only a Good Thing. The best illustration I ever saw on this was in Michael Frost & Alan Hirsch's book *The Shaping of Things to Come,* which I'll leave for you to go discover for yourself.

One of the awkward things about a sizeable church is that it's hard to avoid being flavoured by social culture. I'll explain what I mean. Have you ever been in a formal business meeting, and been caught giggling at an aside? The whole room stops and stares at you. Mortification floods your face as you realise you have flouted a rigidity. You have transgressed against the etiquette of the room.

In Australian society, public speaking events (with the notable exception of Parliamentary Question Time!) tend to carry an expectation that the audience will listen quietly and not be disruptive. Australian Pentecostal preachers, however, like a bit of positive feedback ("Amen! Preach it! That's good!") whereas the New Zealanders scattered throughout their congregations think interjecting is terribly rude. Some churches push gravitas and some push energy. Regardless of the shape it takes, there is a strong social more in church that *proceedings* and *atmosphere* will not be interrupted. They are sacrosanct, and cutting across them would be unthinkable. This does not lend itself to on-the-spot inquiries and explanations, nor yet catastrophes such as fainting deacons or tearful ushers. Few of us stop to remember that we are talking about man-made constructs—made (like the Sabbath) for man, and not the reverse. We are not there to serve the atmosphere. The atmosphere is there to facilitate our connection to God, and nothing else. In that moment where everything is running like clockwork and nobody dare disturb the ambience, is there room for the Spirit to do

His work? Is there room for all the humans present to have human moments with God? Are we clear on what we're there for? Is the congregation there to employ their social heft to support the work of the crew and their runsheet, or is the crew and the runsheet there to support the work of God in the hearts of the congregation? And are the crew not *part* of the congregation, and entitled to full support if lightning strikes?

> *Are the people there for the runsheet, or is the runsheet there for the people?*

Let's not get too hung up on whether or not God can still move: of course He can. He'll move in and around and through us, and sometimes, if He's really intent, right over the top of us. The laughter epidemic of the mid-90s is proof of that. The runsheet is there as a tool to give things a shape to deviate from. Tools are great, if you hold them properly and don't enshrine them. I'm not talking about meetings being hijacked (though occasionally the Spirit will derail things, if He must, to achieve His objectives) but about remembering why we gather in the first place.

When you've got everyone participating, including the simple and the scary, the results are going to be mixed, more often than not. If you're obsessive about your church brand looking good to outsiders, you're going to have trouble being a family; and outsiders, well, half of them will think it's posh and half of them will think it's snobby. In a real family, when your five-year-old comes home with a finger painting, you put it on the fridge. You don't tell them it clashes with the Scandi minimalism and the monochromatic colour scheme. I want to be the kind of parent who, even if my kids were covered in tattoos and metal studs, would still proudly introduce them to my friends. I hope for something of the same rock-bottom love from my church. *Here's Beck* (a little flaky and flighty, but we love her), *and here's the book she wrote* (even though she hardly knew what she was talking about), *she's our girl, isn't she great? Look at her having a go!*

Of course, in a natural family you're only catering for 2–10 people. And now we're back to *is our fellowship too big?* You'd need a mighty big fridge to display all the good works generated in a mighty big church. So you can either scoop up just the cream ("we are proud of this select few only"), or you can, well, build a bigger fridge, so that nobody misses out. The flaw in that argument is that I am still talking in terms of *I will know my church approves of me if they display my finger painting/listen to my ideas/let me give my prophecy.* And there's room in there to argue that there are other ways a church can encourage everyone and let them know that they're approved of, loved, and included—and yes, that they hear from God too. So let's make sure we're paying attention to Column B, even if we can't come at Column A. Be careful not to preach about how everyone's identity is in Christ, and then demonstrate that in the Church, your identity is in fact contingent on your stock value.

I once heard a rumour that a certain church had banned overweight people from its stage team, citing "it encourages an unhealthy lifestyle" as the rationale. I really hope this was nothing but an urban legend, because I'm willing to bet it would have been more about having a slick stage look than anything else. Paul said some rather pointed things to superficial people in Timothy's church in 1 Timothy 2:9, which more or less says, "Let your good deeds be what draws attention, not your cleavage or your highfalutin' fashion sense." We need to be responsible, approachable and amenable. When it comes to our stage team, it's not how fabulous they look, but how fully they love.

My personal opinion is that the more diverse your platform representatives are, the more you reflect the real Kingdom. Here there is neither male nor female, Jew nor Gentile, slave nor free. Jesus didn't just come to save the Beautiful People. If He only wanted to be represented by the Beautiful People, well, He did it wrong, didn't He? His ragtag band of disciples—fishermen! an extortionist! an extremist! that dodgy treasurer! most of them *adults!* and as for the tarts that hang around!—they must have been the laughing-stock of the other rabbis, with their dutiful, scholarly, respectable teenage acolytes. So don't be afraid to include on *your* team all the varieties of people you think God wants to reach with the gospel: short, tall, fat, skinny, young, old, differently-abled, colourful and of all colours. Let all these variegated kinds of people walk or wheel into your church, and see on that stage *someone they can relate to*. Let them see also that little old ladies and dreadlocked young blokes and parents and executives and refugees and students all come together and worship wholeheartedly side by side as a loving and inclusive family.

God loves all *people.*

The church ought to be the one place where externals don't matter. One ought to be able to belong, rank-less and thriving, without having to be fashionable, bright, clear-skinned, fit, suave, moneyed or successful. We should be the oasis for the rustic young Davids in a world obsessed with broad-shouldered, firstborn Eliabs.

I suppose you could make a case that some "body parts" need to be kept private, or internal; but if you're going down that route, remember that those parts are described by Scripture as "essential", and you will need to treat them as such. To be crass about it, the pooper is nobody's favourite body part, and nobody likes what it produces; but if something goes wrong with your pooper, you'll know about it in a big hurry! I fervently hope you don't regard anyone in your congregation this way, though it'll be the rare assembly that doesn't include one. So again, it's going to be a case of finding other ways to let that person know how valued and loved and included they really are—without making them feel poopy!

While we're on the subject of diversity, with all my heart, I want you to think about what will happen when God sends revival amongst the LGBTQ community. God loves all people. These folk are no less loved than you are, and going by 1 Corinthians 6:9–11, no more lost than you were. So He will draw them, as He draws all varieties of people. And when He does, will we be willing to take them in our arms, and lead them to the Cross, where we stand shoulder to shoulder together in our equal need of Him?

I have heard sound arguments on both sides of the gay issue (it's never been a sin/it's always been a sin) and both sides seem to have valid theological reasons for their stance. Therefore, I stand clear of making a dogmatic statement one way or the other, and concentrate on loving the individual people I meet. They are my neighbours. If they accept Christ, they are my family. But if homosexuality happens to be a sin, are we willing to walk with these brothers and sisters and siblings of ours, for years on end if necessary, and be as patient with God's

God has His own pace and priorities within each person's IEP.

transformative process within them, as we want people to be of ours? Or will we demand of them an overnight metamorphosis (or worse, the *appearance* of one) that few of us have ever experienced? Will we be merciful or unmerciful servants? Will we stand by with guidance, yet leave them in peace, so that the Holy Spirit (who, as it turns out, is His own agent) can sanctify them at His own pace and according to *His own* list of priorities within each IEP? A person's orientation may not be the thing God identifies as the most urgent issue for resolution in their life, if at all. It will not be our business to insist that that change first. Think of your biggest and most ongoing character hurdle: how would it feel if you could not be included in the Body until it was resolved? Could you spend years, unaccepted, on the fringe?

I realise that as a lay person, I am not going to be called upon to marry LGBTQ couples, and so my neutrality on this issue is a luxury pastors don't have. All I'm asking is that in every case, we lead with the love of Christ, asking the Holy Spirit to show us what that should look like on the ground in each instance. We might think that shunning is "doing justly" but it is certainly not "loving mercy," and unlikely to be "walking humbly with God," which usually leads us to *empathy* with our fellow humans.

Going back to the subject of imperfect people ministering to one another, I've previously talked about prophecy in general terms. When does a personal prophecy carry weight? Does it depend on the vessel who's giving it? Personally, I look for a sense of resonance, an internal confirmation—this is hard to explain—I'll always give a prophecy a hearing, and if I don't get a "squick" (an uncomfortable twisty something's-not-quite-right-here feeling), a Scriptural conflict, or a complete blank, I'll take it on board. I'm relying on the Holy Spirit to provide the resonance or the squick, but I'm not saying I get it right every time. Prophecy is a good deal more tailored than a sermon, but also more obscure, since it's a message coming through a third party, and can often mean more than one thing.

There *are* times I'm absolutely sure. When it's a visiting preacher who doesn't know me, and their prophecy includes hallmarks from my life—God's fingerprints are all over that thing. It can't be mistaken for a "hallelucination." When it's my own pastor, I listen harder because we both know that they're going to be around to see the results of their words, so they don't speak lightly. I take their advice over a visiting preacher's any day, for the same reason: it's tailored and monitored, they're invested in me. And yet in both cases, I have found much less obscurity and ambiguity in going directly to God for information. This holds true when He chooses not to speak, as well as when He speaks. It's good to encourage people to work on hearing from God for themselves, if they can, rather than being spoon-fed by their ministers or completely reliant on their peers. And yet ... God does ask us to speak to one another! I asked a woman of God once why that was—why, if we were meant to go to the Source, He appoints people with gifts of prophecy in the first place. She said, "Not everyone can hear from God for themselves, or at least not right away." (It helps, of course, if they're listening!) So the function of both the leader and the layperson with the gift of prophecy, is to cover that gap. This goes with the concept of "growing up into the fullness of Christ" being a group project. Frankly, we get by with a little help from our brethren.

I am becoming more and more convinced that God set this up on purpose. I spent a long time in fear of being a "drainer," trying to find the needle of healing in a theological haystack without bothering my poor, overworked pastors. Instead I have found, in middle age, that they appreciate being let in, that they rejoice in using their gifts to bridge and heal. They don't see me as a drain and, far from sighing in resignation when they see me coming, they open their arms and smile warmly. I could take it as far as saying that if I don't let them in, I deny them the opportunity to use their primary gifts. It's no different to a scenario where they might deny me the joy of singing. This is what they do. This is what and how they love. It brings them alive.

Just as God opts to speak to us at times through others, and to welcome prayer even though He knows all things, so He gives us leaders who have the honour and joy of participating in His work. My mother recently wrote a piece in which she points out that olives cannot be eaten straight from the tree: God has left us space to work beside Him. We pick and pickle and press, and then the olive becomes useful in a hundred ways. It is not that He did not foresee that the olive was inedible raw. It is not that our bodies are faulty or fallen because they won't process fresh olive. It is that He delights to bend into partnership with us. He stoops down to make us great. He wears a yoke far below His capabilities, in order to activate ours. And He calls us to be like Him: making room, empowering, accepting help. You heard me: the God of the universe accepts help! Hence the gifts and the office of prophecy; hence the power of prayer; hence the missional movement; hence the re-bodifying of Christ in the Church.

I think, in conclusion, that what we are looking for is *interdependence*, as opposed to *codependence*. We need each other, not for survival (for which Christ alone suffices, for all things are in Him) but for flourishing (for which He has quite pointedly given us one another). He must be First, but He has chosen not to be Only. He cannot (has chosen not to) complete His work in us or in the world without the Body. We can't waste time ranking one another when we've been shown how to empower ("submit to") one another.

There are many excellent books out there on how to do teamwork well, and I'll leave it to you to find them *(cough-Lencioni-cough)*. There

---

We can't waste time ranking one another instead of empowering one another.

is a perception that if we engage in proper teamwork, everything will fall into place. I would just add this caution: get the church culture right at the same time. If you have an entrenched toxic culture, then recruiting everyone *to be toxic together as a team* will only reinforce that toxicity. But if you simultaneously continue to check that the culture is Biblically healthy, or on a trajectory toward health, then gaining allies in that goal is going to pay dividends and achieve traction.

We've touched on knowing the people under us and having real relationship with them. I've heard it said before that "everything goes back to relationship". The trouble with that system is, if you've got a leader who's taken you in dislike, you can't force that person to have relationship with you. And if they won't, you're stuck. If they have bigger fish to fry, your overtures of let's-be-colleagues will fall on deaf ears. And if you're a woman and your leader is a man, they can be very, very reticent to have any sort of relationship with you, mentoring or social. They're probably trying to avoid any hint of impropriety, but from the female point of view, they're merely emphasising the Boys' Club. So when everything goes back to relationship, you can still wind up sitting on the shelf for years, through no fault of your own. I would therefore like to encourage you, as a leader, to bestow healthy, appropriate, boundaried relationship as liberally as you can manage. Treat people as treasures to be discovered, rather than condescending to them. Make sure no one misses out just because they can't access you, or aren't like you, or aren't very likeable.

As always, enquire of the Lord. May He help you see the seed of His image even in the most damaged and stroppy people. May He help you be approachable as well as appropriate. May He make you a light in the darkness. May He make you a magnet of His love, spreading His magnetism to and through all who touch you.

7 Oil Change

THE PENTECOSTAL CHURCH IN AUSTRALIA, speaking very generally, was offered a large paradigm shift in the 90s. In the middle of that decade came the renovated version of the House Church movement: Cell-Based Church. After hearing all the wonders of what could be achieved if we concentrated on small group ministry—enfolding unchurched people lovingly into our world at grass roots rather than yelling at them from some holy sideline—we enthusiastically adopted the idea. The problem was, we were supposed to *exchange* Big Sunday Church for a network of Little Anytime Churches, freeing us up from feeding the Big Beautiful Machine to actually live community lives. But what we did in practice at my church was to *add* Little Church to Big Church—making us twice as preoccupied as before. Once we got Ralph Neighbor's "four Ws" under our belt, it pretty much defaulted back to the insular Home Fellowship model we were all doing in the 80s. Happily, we're starting to look outward once more.

My church is great, but there have been times in the past where I've felt like I existed merely to oil the Big Beautiful Machine. We had the most beautiful machine in town, we felt, and we wanted it perpetuated and perpetuating. No donation of time, money, talent, energy, effort or prayer was too great in its service. At times, that reared far larger than the welfare of those who were going all out to keep it in the style to which it was accustomed. It developed a tendency to chew people up and spit them out.

Don't get me wrong—the thing we are called to is, indeed, far bigger than the welfare of any one of us, because we are part of transforming the world. And yet, God deals with each of us on a heart-by-heart basis and works to make us whole. Our wellbeing is important to Him, and He requires us to love one another. Love will find itself issuing the occasional challenge, or else it is nothing but sentiment; and faith will find itself producing works, or else it is nothing but assent. Somehow, we have to find a balance between the two things, where we are not treating our people like cogs to be burned out and replaced, nor treating them like snowflakes who must never be challenged with work or moral change. Again, it's the correspondence between the Big and Small Pictures. Most churches are probably going to wobble between the two from time to time. We just need to be sure the pendulum never swings too far and gets stuck.

In marriage, there have been times when I've conflated "my husband" with "The Things of my husband". I've gotten preoccupied with resourcing the man, instead of listening to him or spending time with him. With my kids—and a creativity that runs away with me at times—I had to put a sticker on my sewing machine that reminded me to *sow into them* and not just *sew for them*. It can be the same with God: we get caught up in the trappings of Christianity until we are too

We honour God with our service, but we don't serve Service.

Oil Change

worn out to get caught up in Christ. God finds Himself playing second fiddle to The Things of God.

We don't hear too much about the dangers of worshipping Church, or, for that matter, The Vision. To be fair, the line between adherence and idolatry is drawn through each heart, which no one sees but God; but it can be heavily influenced by a culture of fandom. We like our bandwagons (or at least, sanguines and cholerics do!) and we join them with abandon. At one point in my life I had to confess that I wasn't approaching God with the blood of the slain Lamb; instead I'd been bringing Him the vegetables I'd worked so hard on. We honour God with our service, but we don't serve service. We worship God alone, not the things of God—lest we unexpectedly find ourselves worshipping our own efforts.

Incidentally, in my rather dubious personal opinion, I don't think God is terribly invested in the empires we build. So long as the people inside the empires are getting closer to Him, that's likely the main thing He cares about. What we call a particular grouping of those people, or the mass it has, is probably secondary for Him. I've seen huge churches and ministries—structures that we thought would last forever—crumble into dust. Yet you can still find the people who were in them, loving and serving God quite happily in other churches. Why didn't He save the structures from decay? You'll have to ask Him. I don't think it was always corruption. It could have been critical mass. It could have been that they were big ships and He got tired of trying to turn them around. Does God get bored? I don't know. Does He care about your church? Yes, He does (though the building, not so much). But remember that He said *He* would build His church. If He wants to demolish a whole wing of an empire and rebuild it up a different way, He's allowed. Probably, the closer we listen when He says it's time for change, the more we get to participate in the reno and not be broadsided by it. Is the time for change imminent? Ask Him. I suspect so, but I'm not the

Builder. I do know that the prospect of doing church in the exact same inefficient ways, fifty years from now, makes me want to cry and throw things. I respect the magnificent legacy of the past, but don't give me that Ol' Time Religion: God is not a relic, but a living, vastly intelligent Spirit whose experience reaches far into the future as well as the past. Ecclesiastes 7:10 tells us that it's a bad idea to long for the "good ol' days." These are the good *new* days. Let's not insult the new thing that God is doing.

I wonder if maybe Zeal for the House sells more easily than zeal for Jesus. The House is something we can see improving. We can point with admiration and pride to new equipment and refurbishment, a new sound, a new program. We can touch these things. Painting is easier than changing. The rate of renovation in our own souls is harder to track. The degree of closeness to Jesus is hard to quantify, especially if it fluctuates a lot. We can tell our unchurched friends they'll love the decor and music at church. But how do we say things like, "I'm a great deal more patient and good than I used to be"? We want to testify, but we don't want to brag. We can't say, "Come to church and meet Jesus; He'll really help you sort out that mean streak of yours." But we can say, "Come to church and see the Big Beautiful Machine we're building." And we tell ourselves that this bait-and-switch is, after all, for their own ultimate good.

Relevance is a good thing, but not if it goes no further than a musical style or a pair of jeans. What's truly relevant to unchurched people? They want happiness, money, beauty, success, peace, meaning, power, and love. Some of these things they see as prerequisites to the others. We must give them truth, not just what they want, though to a degree the truth will set them free to have some of these things. But let's look for a moment at the assumptions we may be making about our neighbours. Do we think they don't want a God? They throng to action and superhero movies because they want someone to worship who identifies with our weaknesses yet has the power to lift us out of them. Do we think they won't stand for being told how to live? They take it from soap operas, don't they? Do we think they want to be prosaic, independent, self-contained? They love sci-fi movies, which are routinely about discovering things outside ourselves and giving our all, as a team, sometimes sacrificially, in a cause that saves the world. Do we think them selfish or cold? They invest millions in films about flawed people finding unconditional love. Do we think them pragmatic? Deep down they do suspect the Matrix has them, that the world they see is not telling them the full story, and that it cannot tell them who they are.

In short, they are us.

How do we, the people of God, measure success? Do we look at the number of people in our church? That can fluctuate. Some churches sit at the same numbers over a ten-year span, but if the numbers are not comprised of the exact same people, it doesn't mean the church isn't reaching new people, only that populations are transient. Are they new converts or transfers? Of course we want fresh people introduced to Jesus, and if this is not happening we need to change our approach. But none of that means that fostering our transferees is not a real ministry. The real indicator of success is probably this: are the people in the church, whether new or old, moving closer to Christ and His image? Are we kinder, maturer, more faith-filled, humbler, more happily in love with Him than we were a year ago?

(Side note, I have never had much use for the split-haired notion that *joy,* as a Spirit-fruit flavour, is not the same thing as *happiness.* Joy that doesn't produce any happiness is surely meaningless.)

It's not only to the outside that we can sometimes oversell church life. We oversell it to the inside, as well. "Come to this event—it'll change your life!" Well … it may. But it may not—not if we're resistant, or not ready, or if it just doesn't happen to be in our IEP this year. We sing a lot of vivid songs about how free we are, while we continue to enslave our volunteers and interns, and run the congregation ragged. After a while, they turn around and notice that they aren't free at all, and then they have to rethink everything from the ground up. Sometimes it creates sufficient cynicism in people that they leave the church.

> *Anything that creates bondage in people's lives runs counter to the Spirit of Christ.*

Anything that generates bondage in people's lives runs counter to the Spirit of Christ. Being *slaves to righteousness* or *slaves to God* does not have to mean rewardless servitude on a treadmill. We are specifically told in 1 Corinthians 7:23 not to become slaves of humans nor, in Galatians 4:8, to become slaves to the doctrine of "do harder" false believers. Rather, slaves of Christ reflexively do the will of God because we love and trust Him and He takes care of us. God loves a cheerful giver. Each person has to ask themselves if they are serving Christ out of a sense of bondage or out of a sense of gratitude and oneness with Him. And each church has to ask itself if it is encouraging loving service or shackling people to duty. When you're a church leader, you have to pay attention to both of these things.

Finally, I wonder if we continually underestimate the Holy Spirit. Nobody allies themselves with God unless His Spirit draws them. Our prayer should be that He does draw them! It's the Holy Spirit who anoints the music we sing (whether award-winning or basic). It's the Holy Spirit who sends the preacher's words like life-giving injections into hearts. It's the Holy Spirit who fills us with love, power and self-mastery. It's the Holy Spirit who shows us where we need change, who walks with us through flood and fire, stands us on our feet, lays us down beside still waters, and makes our hearts soar. In the end, what we do or don't do in our public services is only one part of the four-dimensional tapestry He weaves in and between all the people in the room and beyond. So while we want to give Him our best, and do all possible to make the central message attractive, in the end it's down to Him, not us. We have the extraordinary privilege of coming along for the ride, and sometimes being allowed to steer.

So talk to God. He won't necessarily take the wheel, but He will certainly navigate, and definitely be at your side. Celebrate the past without enshrining it. Realise that even if the world were to go to wrack and ruin around us, the best in God is yet to come. He's told us so.

8 Safe Kitchens

IN THIS CHAPTER I NEED to touch on some very sensitive issues, and I need to do it honourably. As a survivor of spiritual abuse, it may be that I'll "bleed" a little as I talk about these things. I ask for your grace. I ask that you hear me out, in this, my genuine attempt to give the church a nudge toward a place where these things become less likely.

Most musicians have a bit of melancholy in them. It's the temperament that's given to detail, beauty, order, creativity, perfectionism and even genius at times. Naturally, these traits go hand-in-hand with the arts. I've been singing in church since I was 11 years old. In the church I currently attend, I've served under 12 creative directors across a 29+ year period. (The + matters if it includes the Christmas pageant!) It's a sizeable team in which melancholies and part-melancholies are a majority.

While not always tortured geniuses, melancholies are by nature sensitive souls. It's what helps us make outstanding art: we reflect all the nuances of what it is to be human, manifesting them in song, drama, dance, stories, tech and images. We thrive in an atmosphere that is unhurried, open, explorative, innovative, inspiring and creatively permissive. Room to fail is important, and so is room to succeed.

Room to colour outside the lines is part of that. Melancholies, prizing perfection while living in a far-from-perfect world with their far-from-perfect souls, are also more prone to depression and anxiety than the other temperament types. This makes them more vulnerable than your average churchgoer.

The membership of any large group will filter itself down into smaller social groups. Sometimes, these smaller groups have approaches that come into conflict. Some might be really big on innovation: they become the voice of trendsetting. Some are anxiously copycatting exterior trends. Some like tradition, or nostalgia, mixed in with the new. Others are big on inclusion over talent, and still others on weeding out all the non-excellent people on the bandwagon. All of this clique-forming is perfectly natural, if awkward. The director has the unenviable job of deciding on the overall flavour of the ministry and on which set of ideals are going to be preeminent.

Sometimes, for these and other reasons, things get very tense. This can happen when conflict is open, and it can happen when conflict is suppressed. People get hurt. It can be as small as getting overlooked, or as big as having strips torn off you in front of others. It's the cruel word issued by someone who is untouchable in relation to you. It might be baring your soul and having it dismissed, or a string of small put-downs or other rudenesses. It can be elitism within the team. Sometimes there is the elusive pressure of never being able to please or measure up. You might experience side-eye or blatant bullying. There may be gaslighting as soon as clarification is sought. There can be inexplicable failure to advance, or unfair dismissal. You may be taken advantage of whilst never really being appreciated. Often there is a mismatch between a censure given to one and a free ride given to another. A feeling of being controlled lurks behind your shoulder, along with a mysteriously unpredictable sense of unvoiced approval/disapproval conferred on your friendships or decisions. And because of the power differential

> ## Spiritual abuse
> *is when someone treats you badly,*
> *and gives a religious justification for it.*

between you and your leader, all of these things can constitute spiritual abuse.

Spiritual abuse is, basically, when someone treats you badly and gives a religious justification for it. Technically, it applies to any situation where someone inflicts harm on your spirit; but practically, it occurs mostly during religious mishandling.

If you point out a cruelty and have a verse flung back at you (especially "Touch not the Lord's anointed!") that's spiritual abuse. If you bring up a problem with your leader and are then told that *you are* the problem, that's spiritual abuse. It's red-flagged by what psychologists refer to as *The No Talk Rule,* which contravenes Matthew 5 as it forbids talking to sort things out, seeking clarification, or getting help. For this reason, any order to "shut down all negative conversations" is itself toxic. You can't solve a problem by pretending it isn't there. You'll just wind up with your whole team up to their knees in elephant poo, being asked to call it perfume and on-sell it. Even if your layperson sees a problem you don't believe is there, the proper thing to do is not to dive into defensive denial, but to ask them to unpack it for you, so you can find a way forward together in love.

> *You can't solve a problem*
> *by pretending it isn't there.*

Safe Kitchens

Spiritual abuse can occur between any two people who are using what Adrian Plass calls "specially-sharpened chunks of Scripture" to manipulate one another. You even have to be careful as a parent, when you make appeals based on the Bible to get a desired outcome, to not commit small-scale spiritual abuse. Good: "God asks us to obey our parents." Bad: "God doesn't love naughty little children who disobey their parents." Or even this loathsome gem from *The Simpsons:* "Lies make Baby Jesus cry." If you want a literary example, in *Jane Eyre,* St. John is committing atrocious spiritual abuse toward Jane when he says that her immortal soul is in peril if she does not drop everything, marry him, and go to an early grave on the mission field with him, on no stronger call than his say-so. His sisters rightly shut him down. If you've ever been threatened with the Divine Displeasure for not kowtowing to some human whim, simply because the whim-maker held a position in your church, you've been spiritually abused. If someone who has power over you demands that you open up your soul or life unreservedly to them (such as your Bible college professor requiring you to Friend them on Facebook, becoming privy to your every remark and relationship) that's a degree of Big Brother control that's abusive.

> *In terms of detriment, spiritual abuse is second only to sexual abuse.*

Spiritual abuse is very damaging when it occurs between leadership and laity. Experts say that in terms of detriment, its negative effect is second only to sexual abuse. Let that sink in: second only to sexual abuse. Statistically, it takes two to four years to recover from spiritual abuse once it has ceased. I recommend professional therapy. If you are worried about airing the church's dirty linen before an unchurched psychologist, try to find a qualified Christian one who has no personal stake in your situation. If you're in a small town where stake is non-optional, take heart—many out-of-town psychologists will use Skype.

The most insidious feature of spiritual abuse is that, because the leader is seen as God's delegate—God's Vice Regent On Earth, so to speak—when you're being abused, you can feel that surely God is on the side of His agent, and not on yours. You're the pleb, after all, and several notches down the pecking order. It can be hard to see that *everybody* in the order is getting pecked, and it can be hard to take this stuff to God because you don't see Him as a comfort and an ally, but as an adversary who is ganging up on you with your abuser. You forget that you're a child of God too. The Word cannot comfort you, because it's full of the same knives as those buried in your back, yes? And meantime you have a lot of work to do in remaining a good, forgiving, submissive, teachable Christian, all while having weekly panic attacks on Sunday mornings in the car. It's hard for women because we tire of being submissive when we get the feeling we're not being taken seriously. And it's hard for men because submitting to abuse is such an emasculating thing to go through. And all this while the ever-present help of God seems unavailable! So this strategic tool of the enemy attempts to cut you off from every source of consolation *and* your legitimate—mandated—right to make God your refuge.

> *This strategic tool of the enemy attempts to* cut you off *from your right to* make God your refuge.

When you're being abused, you have to batter your way through all of that if you're to remain close to God. Even then, you find yourself repenting of your poor attitude every five minutes, because you can't help but be angry, frustrated, and in pain. (Take heart: Job couldn't keep a "proper attitude" either, and he was the most righteous man of his time!) It is absolutely grinding to continue to turn up to a team where you are doing your level best to work on your stuff and contort yourself to fit, and you don't see the same reflected, and there seems little reciprocal effort aimed at your welfare. The years go by, one hope-filled, promising new year bleeding miserably across the finish line into the next, while nothing improves in the entrenched *Animal Farm* system of *some animals are more "equal" than others.* You wonder who is paying you to remain on this nail-studded treadmill, but you don't feel free to leave, because you've been taught that *you never leave while things are bad.* And surely these people, who claim to be so much closer to God than you are, know something you don't. It makes you second-guess yourself, your beliefs, the heart of God who has appointed this person to the position they're hurting you from, and the people above that who appear to be allowing it to continue. You don't want to be that person who quits when the going gets tough. You don't want to miss whatever lesson God is trying to teach you, lest you have to "go around the mountain again" at a later date. If your abuser is high up the chain of command, you don't feel safe reporting them, for the same reasons you don't feel safe praying: you think you're the only one in your corner, and that complaining is unrighteous. You are literally caught between The Rock and a hard, hard, hard place.

None of this looks good to the world, and it gets harder to hide as time goes by, especially if you have done what was asked of you and acquired real, honest friendships with unsaved people. No matter how little you tell them, they can plainly see that serving God is torturing you. God may even send you one of these unchurched people to jolt

Safe Kitchens

you out of your mystical dilemma with a simple dose of common sense: *get out!* So you don't want to leave because the going got tough. But when the going gets *poisonous,* it can be smarter to leave. It's whether or not you feel personally that God is releasing you to do so. In the end, you're *His* servant, and nobody else is allowed to judge you.

When we talk about the logistics of serving God in an organisation or church department, we look hard at the risks, and then we look at what it is we feel God wants us to do, and proceed with both joy and caution. Everyone knows that the music ministry, filled with egos both fragile and inflated, can have a dark side—or at least that sensitive people (which is most creatives) are going to experience some of it as dark at some point. You know you're going to get offended in church from time to time, because humans are there, and you're one of them. That's par for the course. What you don't expect is to wind up in therapy. You don't expect to have to explain, red-rimmed again, to your six-year-old—against the evidence of their own eyes—why serving God in church is still the best thing ever. An incident is just an incident, but repeated incidents are patterns of bullying. A systemic culture of these incidents being regarded as "perfectly fine" constitutes a toxic environment.

It's tempting to say, "If you can't take the heat, get out of the kitchen!" But whoa. Whoa, there, Neddy. Why is the kitchen so unsafe in the first place? Who's running this kitchen, the Soup Nazi? Aren't we supposed to be *counter*cultural?

I'm a woman, and we don't walk alone at night. In fact, women get assaulted in broad daylight just jogging in the park in their track suits. But does that mean I must a) never wear sweats, b) never jog, c) never go to the park, day or night, d) never leave the house, or e) pretend I'm a man? Is it my fault, if I get raped in the park at two in the afternoon because the park isn't safe? Whose responsibility is it to ensure that our parks are safe spaces? Mine? No. It's the responsibility of the lawmakers, law upholders, and law enforcement.

Whose responsibility is it to ensure that spaces are safe to serve in?

In the same way, it's not good enough to say that sensitive snowflakes should stay off the worship team, lest they not withstand the spiritual abuse we've normalised within it. Keep sensitive people out of the arts? You won't have anyone left! And it's not up to *me* to make sure the team is safe to join and serve on. It's up to the leadership and the policies.

Abuse doesn't only happen in creative teams, of course. It happens in any arena where one person has perceived power over another. Wherever a discriminatory threat is possible—ostracision, the withholding of opportunities, labelling—the risk of abuse must be neutralised, or at least mitigated.

When abuse occurs, it's unpastoral to engage in victim-blaming, trying to minimise the abuser's bad behaviour by pointing out flaws in how the victim handled it, or how they enabled it, or weren't strong or holy enough to stand there and take it like a punching bag, or came in bruised to start with. Few of us would take the attitude that just because a person is bruised, a few more bruises oughtn't to be pinned on us: that would be like saying, "If you're going to run over a pedestrian, be sure to point out in court that they were already disabled." Instead, we protect the least of these, if we indeed see bruised people as "the least".

It's difficult, as a lay person with a ministry, to tread the fine line between "submitting to your pastor" and "feeling owned". Many gifted people take their gifts, and maybe even themselves, outside the church, either because they're not a welcome gift, or because the rules of gift-operation within the church are (rightly or wrongly) too stringent for them. Occasionally, a leader will exercise a degree of control by which they deign to permit or expressly forbid a person to pursue their God-given ministry. When this happens, what they're actually doing is *asking the person to serve two masters.* Ultimately, they can either obey the God who called them, or they can obey the leader who is trying to un-call them. It's either the Master or the pastor. We mustn't ever tempt them to stick with one and resent the other. It puts them in an impossible bind, because God has asked us to honour our leaders. God in turn honours this obedience, but He will not let anyone take advantage of it indefinitely. Remember, all three parties are meant to be on the same side!

On rare occasions a Svengali-like situation evolves. The leader appropriates the person's gift, holds veto on their opportunities, and dangles permission like a carrot. They then take it a step further and persuade the person to believe that only with *their* covering and within *their* parameters will the person be successful, or used of God, or remain in the will of God. The hostage is then ordered to develop Stockholm Syndrome post-haste, or face the consequences. When this happens, the leader has actually usurped the role of God in the person's life. They have called themselves the source, the author and perfector. What you have in that instance is not a church at all, but a cult.

Something that sails very close to the wind of spiritual abuse is the idea of *testing people out.* God tests people, yes, but He's God, and the One who loved us enough to face the Cross for us, so He's allowed. Peter tested Sapphira, but he didn't *engineer* the situation, it just unfolded. I don't think we can make that a precedent for the kind of testing I'm about to discuss. Paul does tell Timothy to *look into* potential deacons, and this is sometimes translated "test"; but the word here, *dokimazo,* leans equally toward "approve them before you appoint them," and is also rendered in English with terms such as *discern, prove, examine.* It's not necessarily about *setting* them an exam—it could just as soon be about observing how they handle the exam that is life. It should never be about entrapment. We don't pray "Lead us not into temptation," and then turn around and tempt others.

There's an idea in Christian service that you should be willing to do anything that needs to be done in the church—not turning your nose up at menial tasks, but being humble, obedient, and proactively helpful. So far, so good. You don't want a church full of people who are too good to maintain it, or who play the "that's not my ministry" card every time a gap needs filling. But there's also this sly idea: that you don't get to do the thing you really want to do—the thing you feel called to— unless you've passed through some hazing or initiation ritual of doing the things you *don't* want to do and *aren't* called to.

I have a bit of a problem with this, and having served under so many leaders in one particular place might account for some of it; you get tired of having to prove yourself again and again and again with each change of management. Everyone serves an apprenticeship; but *how many* apprenticeships must one person serve, before they are declared fit to stand? I understand that a leader might want to see what I'm made of. I understand that toilets won't clean themselves, and I don't mind doing that. I understand that small jobs build the skills in you for bigger jobs, and that this is often God's path for us. If a pastor feels in God that they need to direct someone this way, so be it.

It's the random, not-God schemes I take issue with. I hate the idea that a person who knows very well what God wants them to do and has gone and gotten equipped, might be deliberately side-tracked, sometimes at apogee, into something irrelevant to their calling—just so someone else on a power trip can rub their hands together and see whether they'll baulk. I find that really, really manipulative. I would go so far as to call it *playing head games*. We ought not to play lightly with other people's psychology, nor with their destiny. You don't cut

Safe Kitchens

> *Don't test anyone you wouldn't go to the Cross for.*
> *It's repugnant to perform experiments on people God has asked us to look after.*

people open to see what colour they bleed. They'll bleed sooner or later anyway, and who knows? they might bleed blue! And there is no reason why a square peg ought to be left in a round oubliette for any longer than necessary. If you are tempted to test people as God tests them, a good rule of thumb would be *don't test anyone you wouldn't go to the Cross for.* It's repugnant to perform experiments on people God has asked us to look after.

The *fallout* from spiritual abuse can last a lot longer than the 2–4 years it takes to *recover* from it. My case back then was fairly mild, as these things go, and until recently I was *still* observing fallout from it, despite my best attempts to forgive and forget. I had to have expert help from trained prayer ministers in dismantling bitter roots, ungodly coping structures and inner vows, repenting of judgment and the forming of expectancies, and of conflating God with man.

Spiritual abuse poisons your ability to trust. It puts a stumbling block between you and every leader you encounter going forward, because in your experience, leaders are *untrustworthy* and *looking for ways to keep you down.* Changes in personnel bring an excruciating, soaring mix of ardent hope and abject terror. You have to do the whole spiritual gymnastics thing each time: "This person is not that person. God is on all of our sides. That was then, this is now. We are allowed to talk about the elephant in the room, if there is one. God can redeem any situation and bring life to you. You're not alone. Calm your farm."

Safe Kitchens

I talked in a previous chapter about leaders approaching their congregation with suspicion. Now I must confess that—obviously—I have been among those who approach their leaders with suspicion. Me and God, we do a lot of hand-clutching. It's been hard for me to trust God with the leaders He puts over me, because I'm conscious that He's running His own agenda, balancing the needs of everyone in the church AND its mission. But I want to, and I'm grateful to be back in a position where I can choose to. I know that some of the future is bound to include stretching for me. I say *stretching*, while hoping it won't be the rack again. It's hard for me to trust those who employ these leaders without first projecting what they'll be like to work under—though I recognise that a few appointees are, unfortunately, two-faced. I mean no malice by this; it is merely an observation.

The vast majority of leaders I've met have been wonderful and gifted people who've enriched my life; they don't have to be perfect for me to love them. But when they have power over me—when they hold my ministry in their hand to lift, squeeze or drop—I proceed with caution, knee-jerk style. Maybe that's just sensible; maybe it indicates I still have work to do; maybe it's a hangover from my New Zealand upbringing (we come out of the womb sceptical). Maybe all three. I have found that if there's nothing I want, the fear abates: if perchance they wished to take something from me, there's nothing to take. But it's a great pity as a Christian to have to resort to a Buddhist approach. And it's a long way from operating in faith. Again, I'm thankful for the time people have taken to let me heal, and for putting spiritual tools in my hands to repair damage and keep up some preventive maintenance. I have no problem trusting my current crop of leaders, nor my beautiful God. It is a work begun in me, not yet finished, but oh, the relief at having begun!

You are quite free at this point to conclude that I have too much baggage for my testimony to have credence. But consider that your congregation is likely to include a few people who've been through similar things. It's most definitely going to include people who've been hurt. It's not productive to dismissively note that "hurt people hurt people," because the corollary there would be, "so stay away from those losers". And that's probably not what you're called to do. You may well be called to lift the "losers" to win with you.

One more word about spiritual abusers. They are not always bad people. Often they love the Lord passionately but are perpetuating damage done to themselves, or are non-empathetic, deceived, or simply heedless. Occasionally they are people whose neurological processes are atypical and who are baffled at why their every good intention and communication seem to go awry. It's possible to do bad while meaning well: it happens to all of us from time to time. I'm not saying that makes it okay. I'm saying that we can make accurate judgments about the behaviour, without stepping over the line and judging the character. It's the difference between *appraisal* and *condemnation*. So do pray for them. Pray for them to receive the very blessings you're asking God to give you. Do forgive them. Know that God is forever working in their life and will not give up. If pop star Kesha can bring herself to sing about the victory of forgiveness in her song "Praying," you can too, eventually. But do look after yourself, and do cling to the hand of Jesus, and do get help.

Forgiveness does **not** *mean putting yourself back in their hands.*

Forgiveness does *not* mean putting yourself back in their hands; it merely means cancelling your side of the debt. And if you leave, go

Safe Kitchens

> **Codependency** *is when I expect* **you** *to work harder on* **my problem** *than I do.*

gracefully, and speak the truth in love if you can. If you stay, may God have mercy on your soul, you're in for a rough ride; but God is with all of you and will work all things for good for all parties in His own inscrutable, long-range way. I can't tell you which decision is for you. I'm not even sure I made the right one all those years ago. But having made it, God has brought me invaluable lessons out of it, lessons I would not want to be without. This chapter is my attempt to share a little of those lessons in the hope that you can avoid becoming or serving under an abuser.

It's only fair to add that if you've been in leadership for a while already, you've likely been in for some spiritual abuse yourself, from desperate people who expect you to solve all their problems. You can't, and it's unfair on you. I've had times where I've thought of asking my pastor to pray for me, and then remembered that I've barely prayed about it myself. Isn't the definition of *codependency* when I expect *you* to work harder on my problem than *I* do? You can't wave a magic wand over forty years of someone else's pain and make it all better through the strength of your love for them. You can't even eat at their house with any regularity, even if you want to. The bigger your church, the less likely it is that you will, even once. And yet you will probably be bombarded with Shoulds. Pastor, you should do this. Pastor, we should do that. With the veiled hint all Shoulds have: that if you *really* cared, if you were *really* a woman of God, you'd *do* something. You might have to remind hurting folk like me that their prayers of faith are just as powerful as yours, or you'll need superpowers to meet the outrageous expectations some of us have. Some will try to bully you and emotionally manipulate you, whether out of arrogance or pain. It's going to take all your love and His to respond to that with grace and firmness. Knowing your core business and your calling will be vital, because sometimes they'll be right—and sometimes they won't.

Talk to the Lord. Ask Him to help you recognise dangerous situations, both for yourself and for your flock, in a timely manner— and to deal with them well. Ask Him to give you the grace to make any changes necessary. Ask Him for wisdom, which He freely promises to all comers, and for discernment to get to the truth of things, and for the dexterity to impart that truth lovingly. May love and faithfulness never leave you.

I'm aware that I have been talking about some pretty heavy stuff and I haven't wrapped it up nicely in a neat bow yet. Expect bows in the last chapters!

9 Eagles, Shields & Pedestals

MOST CHURCHES HAVE A HIERARCHY, if numbers permit. There'll be a presbytery of some sort, or an eldership with a first-among-equals, or a senior pastor flanked by assistant pastors, maybe departmental heads, elders, deacons, and so forth. Often there's a Board who make the major decisions, including hiring the pastoral staff. There's always a cadre of leaders and then a congregation. I do wish sometimes it was more like the Round Table, but even that was a leadership team and not the whole nation.

It's tempting to think that since Paul asked the church to honour leaders, that they were always Way Up There while everyone else was Way Down Here. In fact, he wouldn't have had to say a thing if that had been the case. Paul describes himself as the battered old retainer bringing up the rear and taking all the nonsense. He knows people describe him as a paper tiger: "Looks good on parchment, but can't preach to save his life; mate, he'll put you to sleep—one bloke fell out the window!" (This encourages me greatly, as I am also much better at writing than preaching, despite being able to talk for hours!)

When I was working as a school chaplain, I was introduced to the word *panopticon:* a term used in pedagogy to describe the teacher's

Eagles, Shields & Pedestals

physical location in the classroom—being able to watch all of the students at once. It denotes "being above" them physically, so that you can keep an eye out for behaviour and attention that needs flagging. It reminded me immediately of the high-placed pulpits in magnificent traditional churches (most likely so placed to allow the voice to carry, rather than out of any eagle-eyed suspicion). The classroom teacher occupies the panopticon and keeps a tight rein on things, lest chaos ensue. And while it's true that a class even of well-behaved kids will certainly and rapidly run amok when unmonitored, the church shouldn't be seen in the same light or from the same distance. The prefix *ped-*, as in *pedagogy* and *pediatrician*, means *child*. We, the congregation, are not recalcitrant children. The church is (ostensibly) filled with New Creations—adults—and our natural fleshly desire to run amok is being gradually transformed out of us by the Holy Spirit. Or, if you want to stick with the *children* idea—in relation to the wisdom of God, even the oldest and mightiest preacher on earth is still a *child* of God, and therefore a peer looking through a tinted window beside us.

It's worthwhile noting that the panopticon was originally designed for a limited staff to watch prison inmates in such a way that the inmates were never sure if/when the warden's eye was on them, leading to a measure of prisoner self-regulation. This idea was picked up for asylums as well. That's right, folks. Panoptica are for keeping *prisoners and the mentally ill* in line. So unless this describes your congregation … I'll just leave this here …

I once did a course in which an idea was included that went like this: *If you've got a high calling, you've got a high cost. Great eagles fly alone.*

Now, the teacher of this course was a fantastic guy who is doing fantastic things for God—like, seriously fantastic. And it's true that there are definite costs attached to such a calling, as well as incredible joys, and he's experienced both. I don't think he still believes great eagles fly alone, though he's had his lonely days. It seemed even back then, no offence and no arrogance intended, a flawed philosophy that I didn't see reflected in Scripture. Perhaps it was meant more as an observational warning than a job requirement—that you wind up leaving behind a lot of friends whose dedication can't keep up with yours.

I don't think it's terribly healthy to strike a pose, grip our lapel and declaim, like Uncle Andrew in *The Magician's Nephew*, "Ours, my boy, is a high and lonely destiny." A destiny shouldn't be high and lonely by design, even if by default. God always intended us to be in community, in relationship and in humble accountability with others. Jesus had a fan base but He also had twelve good friends, three of which were besties, and the family at Bethany where He went to relax. These friends had each other and their families. Paul had Timothy, Barnabas, Silas, Priscilla, Aquila and John Mark—not to mention all the other people he addressed as peers. Going back, Moses had Zipporah, Aaron, Jethro, Joshua and Caleb. David had a bodyguard of 30 and still couldn't keep out of trouble.

God always intended us to be in community.
The more isolated *you are,*
the more at-risk *you are.*

The more a leader is isolated in a lofty place, the more at-risk he is. The more he sees himself as elite, outside of the congregational world, the more he will feel himself entitled to break rules the congregation must keep, and that's how pastors wind up having affairs. (Well, not the only reason, but a part of it that bears looking at.) It might also be true that if he identifies too strongly with the congregation and sees that they let themselves cheat a little, he might jealously permit himself to cheat a little too. The reverse is definitely true. And nobody is bulletproof; nobody. .

From time to time you may be tempted to ask for, or demand, loyalty from those you lead. I personally do not believe in loyalty to a human individual. It too easily bleeds over into idolatry. I believe in honour, and I believe in faithfulness, and I believe in fealty to Jesus my King.

To begin with, loyalty can never be demanded: it must be earned. While ostensibly a person can *demonstrate* a loyalty, they can't be commanded to *feel* one. Leaders who demand an outer show regardless of inner conviction—or reciprocation—have missed the mark and do not deserve such devotion. Any leader who argues that a person should keep their mouth shut/toe the line/suck it up for the Sake of the Church has completely missed what a church is: a family who goes all out to protect and nurture every member without exception.

Loyalty to a church or leader can be a dangerous thing that keeps people in bondage to toxic relationships and systems. In some senses it is like Stockholm Syndrome, where a kidnapped person is brainwashed into allegiance. Do not mistake loyalty for faithfulness. *Loyalty* is an ally of jealousy, where *faithfulness* is an ally of honour and gratitude and love. The only being who can safely and integrously wield jealousy is the Most High God, because He knows that His love not only exceeds all others, but is our ultimate completeness. His jealousy is born of His love, whereas our jealousy tends to be born of our insecurity, pride or greed.

All of these alternatives to loyalty—honour, faith, fealty—belong to God first. He is the one we honour, put our faith in, are faithful to, owe allegiance and life to. Psalm 89:14 says that righteousness [judgment] and justice are the foundations of His throne, with love [mercy, loving kindness] and truth [faithfulness] emanating from it. 1 John 1:5 says that God is light. Ephesians 5:9 says that the fruit of the light consists in all goodness, righteousness and truth.

To sum up:-

Loyalty: "I will have a blind and dogged devotion to you, regardless of what you're like. I will have your back no matter how wrong you are."

Honour: "I will respect and defend you, in accordance with truth and duty. I will have your back when you are right. When you are wrong I will lovingly and privately tell you the truth."

Faithfulness: "I will always be there for you, and believe in you and your potential. I will have your back in prayer. When you are wrong I will keep loving you, and trust God to steer you right."

Fealty: "I will always put God above every other priority in my life, including you, for you may on occasion be wrong, and I love you best when I love Him first."

So, then, our fealty is first of all to the light-filled One who embodies truth, justice, mercy, goodness and righteousness. Not to any of His representatives, necessarily—not if they stray from the path of those things. Not to our country or family or firm or church or old school tie or team. The highest allegiance is always on the side of truth and justice, regardless of pre-existing relationships.

From time to time, leaders will appear who will try to claim instant loyalty, demanding that we side with them or bow to them. Never be one of them. You are not a demigod, right? People do not have to side with you if you are not on the side of truth. They belong to God, not to you. If you go off the rails, they are not obligated to fall in line with anyone who denies the fruit of the light, or who produces bondage and darkness. They do have to uphold you with hope, faith, and love,

I love you best when I love Him first.

which means having your back in prayer. But unless it is a prison you're running, nobody should be lining up to be in your special cadre of protected pawns. Let's just not go there. Don't ask for loyalty. Look instead for faithfulness, and reward it when you see it.

You, dear leader, are a person with the call of God on your life. So am I, but yours is "a noble task." For both of us, there is a subtle trap we must avoid: worshipping the Call instead of the Caller.

I am tempted to worship the call when I throw all my energy into doing what God has asked of me, to the detriment of beholding and loving and talking to Him. If I glorify my call—"look at me, I'm Callllled! I'm Anoooiiinted!"—more than I pay attention to my character, I'm in danger of crashing and burning at the wheel. Worshipping the call can also look like putting its trappings before the other important responsibilities God has given me, such as caring for my family.

This is a very tough issue, but it becomes less tough when you remember that, like the congregation, like the lost, those closest to you are really in the same category: *people who rely on me to minister to them.* Hard questions await missionaries who must decide whether or not the field is the right place for their children, or whether or not *now* is the right time for the field, or whether one child's nature necessitates a choice that wouldn't be right for a different child. At 16 on the field, dying of social homesickness, my parents gave me the choice of staying on the field with them, going to an American boarding school in the capital, or going home to New Zealand to board. None of those choices were perfect, but still I honour them for giving their lives in sacrificial service to the Lord. I went home to New Zealand. For a different family, the choice could have been to simply not go on the field until their kids had graduated. I can't say which is the better course because I do believe my parents made an obedient choice by going. That doesn't make it the right choice for everyone.

In pastoral ministry it's going to look more like answering the question, "How much of *my family's* time will I give my call?" Because it's not just your time. In some sense (especially a federal sense) your (singular) ministry is your (plural) ministry. That is not to say that the family can't have input into the call's boundaries. Make time for their sporting events or recitals or dinner conversation or individual ministries. Make sure they count as people. They, too, are your missionfield.

The gifts and call of God are without repentance. He doesn't withdraw His enabling. But they are always meant to be conducted in the light of the whole counsel of the Word of God—that Word which encourages us to love God with all we are, to love ourselves, to equally love our neighbour, to love and respect our spouse, and to bring up our children in such a non-exasperating way that they stay close the Lord.

We talked in an earlier chapter about being entitled. I think it's worthwhile here to bring up, literally, titles.

I generally don't use titles in church, unless I'm explaining someone's role or job description. Remember, I am a lay person, coming from a lay person's perspective. I can't remember ever addressing someone as "Pastor" in place of their proper name—"Thank you, Pastor"—any more than I would have said "Thank you, Plumber," or "Thank you, Shopkeeper." I don't use "Brother" or "Sister" either, because they feel contrived: if I regard you as a sibling, you'll know it. I don't refer to my pastors in conversation as "Pastor Firstname" or "Pastor Lastname", except in certain specific situations where protocol comes into play and I need to be obedient to it. In regular life, it just smacks so much of the pedestal. My pastors are not vain people, nor are they distant or formal. So why would I wish to address them or refer to them with a rank? The only time people do that in real life is in America, where they rather stiltedly say "Doctor" or "Officer"; or in the armed forces, where you might hear "Captain" and so on, but even then, "Captain Barnes" sounds to me like "Postman Pat" and I have trouble saying it with a straight face.

Jesus specifically asked us not to request titles. It's one of the many things He said that we gloss over. A title, I guess, goes a long way to describe the function we have in the church. Yet I cannot conceive of going about saying, "How're you doing today, Sound Man Steve? What's new, Usher Jones? Nice shoes, Life Group Leader!" and so forth. It's just so artificial. If we're going to describe function, it would be better to drop the grand old curlicued title of *Pastor* and call it what it is, The *Looking After People* Person.

Here's the truth: pastors, like all people, are going to be human beings who make mistakes. And when they do, it's far, far easier for me to forgive them and support them, if I love them as human beings who make mistakes. It's really hard to forgive "The Pastor". Thinking of that person as *the embodiment of a title* creates hierarchy and distance in my head. I lose sight of the fact that all of us stand, with our stuff, ankle-deep in the blood of Jesus before the Throne. Nobody in that lineup is exempt from the need for it: not the person whose job is pastoring who, when he wrongs me, I feel superior to; nor me, the person who is constantly stumbling and crashing and who feels so inferior at times to all other people.

*Respect the office;
but love the person.*

To see you, my leader, as a *person*, is to accord you more honour and far more love, than I can if I merely see you as a title bearer. I can respect your office, I can salute your uniform (so to speak), but it is not respect that marks us as children of God—it is love. And I cannot love a plaque. You may find your badge a useful tool to keep that little bit of separation going between yourself and your congregation, but to what end? I can understand you wanting a titular reminder that final decisions are yours. I can understand you guarding your privacy. But if it's merely distance for the sake of stature, that's quite a different thing.

Sooner or later, you're going to do or say something that I'm uncomfortable with or annoyed by. That's just life. A couple of responses are available to me. I can grumble at your position: "A pastor should do better than that." Or I can be gracious to your personhood: "Joe's had a tough couple of months, and the best way I can extend God's love is to give him some space & grace." Denigrating or venerating the office is one thing; loving a friend is another thing entirely. So if I leave off your title when I address you, that's not disrespect, it's warmth. It tells you I think of you as family. In fact, I wonder how much conversations and attitudes would change if we stopped saying "the Church" altogether, and instead referred to "the Family"?

Throughout human history, humankind has made many efforts to distance itself from God. And God's response is always the same: He takes steps to close the gap. So if the God of the Universe wants a bunch of suburban housewives and tradies and young professionals and kids and old codgers and homeless people seated with Him in heavenly places, it seems to me that loftiness, as a trait, is not that important to Him. God is the Most High. His Son has the Name above all Names: "God Saves". Yet He calls us up. He moves close. He is quite literally *down-to-Earth*. And He asks us to emulate Him.

The rarefied air above the touch of the common man can all too quickly go to one's head or cause an attitude of martyrdom, but you can probably read about that in pretty much any leadership book off the shelf. Just remember that while you are doing your Great Eagle thing, you need not deny yourself the compassion and support of church members who sincerely want to have your back. I guess you need to be twice as careful as the average Christian in choosing an accountability partner. Don't be afraid to have friends, though. Don't be afraid to be known. There's safety in numbers. And there's respect in transparency, even if you're not too proud of certain things. I guess it's going to come down to gauging who can handle what. You don't want to make any one person your *sole* friend, or tempt them into a soul tie; don't offer them the throne. Just don't set out trying to handle everything on your own. You're a body part. The hand might wear the rings, but it can't do much unless it's attached to the arm. Even eagles need a wingman. It's important to remember that *your skills* are not God's gift to the church: *you* are. And they are also His gift to you. Don't just be a leader. Be a person.

Your skills are not God's gift to the church: you are.

One of the most contentious and misunderstood passages in the Bible is Ephesians 5:22: "Wives, submit to your husbands." This follows closely on the heels of "Submit to one another out of reverence to Christ" and is not far behind our earlier passage about ministry functions. There's a strong current in church history around *submitting to your leaders*.

The best exposition I've ever heard on this issue is by Anne Hamilton in her book *God's Panoply*. The Greek word for "submit", *hupotasso*, does indeed mean *to be subordinate*. But the surrounding language (which is important, because Paul weaves concepts together poetically through both Greek and Hebrew to ensure that meaning is underscored and not lost in translation) indicates that the word of choice would have been the Hebrew *nasa'*, for which there wasn't a parallel Greek term available. *Nasa'* is all about being an armour-bearer, a concept closely allied to the role of the *paraclete*. It's partnership and covenant. It's about having someone's back, the way Jonathan's aide said, "Your call; I am with you, heart and soul." It's related to *nissi*, banner, *that which is lifted up*. So when Paul tells us to *submit* to one another, he doesn't mean that one should push the other down. He means that one should lift the other up. It's probably related to *hupsoo,* "If I be *lifted up* from the earth". And that changes the whole meaning and thrust of Paul's admonishment. There's no cowering, no standover tactics. There's no coercion. There's no demeaning. There's no sexism. There's only supply and support and protection, and going by the previous verse, it's reciprocal. Even if it *weren't* going both ways, if we note that the wife has been asked to be Backup & Logistics, we also see that the husband has been asked to be Bodyguard. He's the one who'll take the bullets. How 'bout that mutuality now …?

Far from throwing your weight around, you need to allow yourself to be supplied and supported and protected by the Bride, even as you supply, support and protect her. By "supported" I don't mean you should lie back on silken cushions in a pavilion, while slaves fan you with giant fluorescent feathers. I mean you should not disdain the offers of the people God puts around you. Historically, there's been a lot of emphasis on not permitting the ministries of church members to

> "Submission" doesn't mean that one should push the other down.
> It means that one should lift the other up.

become "Lone Ranger" outfits—all while the man at the top is himself a Lone Ranger!

Like Chief Vitalstatistix in Goscinny & Underzo's *Asterix* comics, let your people have the honour of bearing you up on your shield of faith. Let them have a part to play. Be in relationship with them as first among equals, not as sage among savages. Vulnerability is not weakness. In fact, it is the key to the kind of empathy that should characterise Christian love and leadership. I would far rather build community with a leader who is willing to receive from me as well as pour into me. U.S. President Woodrow Wilson once said, "You cannot be friends upon any other terms than upon the terms of equality." I think there's truth there. Jesus referred to His disciples as friends—those He trusted to obey the Father's words that He'd brought them. He sought their moral support shortly after, in Gethsemane. Yes, it's humbling to need people—but it's good enough for the Son of God! Are we friends? I am grateful for mentors, but I avoid conversations where my input is rated at nil. If I can't contribute, I instinctively want to leave. Perhaps that's immaturity, or pride; yet all people want to feel valued, and having one's remarks ignored gives the opposite effect. It makes one feel pointless.

Some of these people will be smarter than others; that's okay. You don't have to *obey* them. You just have to *value* them, and let them know their contribution matters. Give them dignity, even if they talk rubbish. Sometimes this is more important than the automatic work ethic which says, "I must not take advantage of these good folks." The poor, hard-pressed Macedonian churches, seeing need and vision in other parts of the Body, *begged* Paul to let them be part of the solution. There's a difference between using people, and allowing God to use people. It's not always kind to reject encouragement simply because you know who you are in Christ and the opinions of others aren't relevant to you. And sometimes blessing people is as simple as accepting a vegetable lasagne or a compliment.

Talk to God about these things. Ask Him to help you avoid the traditional pitfalls of gold, girls and glory, but also of the kind of pride or reverse pride which sets you apart in loneliness instead of holiness. It is not good for a human to be alone, even with the presence of God for daily company, even in an unfallen Eden. Since we are far from Eden, ask Him to help you choose wisely who to lean on and listen to on each occasion.

10 And For My Next Trick ...

... I WILL NEED A BEAUTIFUL ASSISTANT, or three, or thirty, or three hundred. I mentioned at the outset of this book that I have two children, aged 18 and 20 as of this writing. One of them is more insistent than the other. I have never been able to explain to her satisfaction that "some people have more authority than others, and God's made me yours; you need to obey me because I'm your mother." To her, this sounds like, "Because I said so." I cannot adequately answer her response, "Does that mean you're *superior?* That you're Way Up Here and I'm Way Down There? Does it mean I don't matter and what I want doesn't matter?"

Traditionally, the answer has been, "Do as you're told and don't answer back." This hasn't worked for my daughter, and I'm not sure if this is because of her IEP, her generation or her temperament. I know I hated being shut down, so maybe it's a mistake I'm trying to avoid, rather than a principle I'm failing to apply. My kids believe they're valid members of this family with valid things to input. Traditional answers for these issues go, "Eat what you're given, and if you want to call the decor, pay rent or get your own place." The buck stops with Chris and I, and fortunately, we're the ones with the bucks.

Maybe I'm a weak parent, but I'm not satisfied with my kids finding their home dissatisfying, a place to escape from. We all matter. My kids aren't *waiting to become* people: they *are* people.

Generalising, Generation Z appears to like interaction. They've never known a world without devices. They're social media-savvy, used to putting their voices out into the world. They obey their teachers but they don't go quietly. Even with authority, things now go more smoothly when they're interactive, negotiable, flexible, and communicated both ways—much more egalitarian and explained than dictatorial or obscure. They want to engage with concepts as they're learning, and have opportunities to give feedback. They have been fed self-esteem to the back teeth and come out believing they matter.

> *Young people are* not
> *"the church of tomorrow".*
> *They're the church of* today.

We can go on bending each new generation of Christians into our 70s model of "because I said so," and they will probably capitulate out of reverence for Christ. But will they be happy, or free—or merely repressed? We can go on enforcing "that's the way we've always done it" regardless of its obsolescence. We can play "Simon Says" until Jesus comes back, but will we get optimal results? I think not. As has long been said, children are *not* "the church of tomorrow"—they're the church of TODAY. And so, with barely any research, and a heaping helping of hubris, let me present a few harebrained ideas for your delectation: how do we future-proof our young congregants?

In therapy, professional care and design, there's a trend nowadays toward what's called *client-led solutions.* Research shows that people in need of help, absorb that help better when they can direct it somewhat. It becomes less about giving a man a fish, or even teaching him to fish, and more about asking him where the fish are. It gives the client back their agency. They are not at the mercy of systems, nor passive recipients, but treated like adults who know themselves a little. The client takes much more ownership of treatment when they've had a hand in prescribing it. Every counsellor knows that it's better, by using careful questioning, to let a client dig a custom-made answer out of themselves, rather than impose a solution upon them. An ounce of insight into your own capabilities is worth a pound of external advice. The trick as the counsellor is to ask the Holy Spirit to help you guide the conversation.

I would like to see more of this in church. While we can't poll the people for every little decision we make, we can't *sheeple* them either. We don't have to operate like we are the only people with answers. When God gives you a sizeable group of people, filled with His Spirit and gifts both natural and spiritual, pool your resources. We spend a lot of time *telling* these gifted people what God is saying, and not enough time *asking* them what God is saying. That is, after all, what their spiritual gifts are given for. God hands out jigsaw pieces to all of us, and we don't get around to looking at them because we aren't running an *each-of-you* model of church. When the member brings their burden or idea to our attention, instead of saying, "That's good,

---

We spend a lot of time telling people what God is saying, instead of asking them what God is saying.

but it's not what God is doing here in this season," perhaps it might be worth considering that *maybe it is* and that *this is the proof.*

In a natural family, we start out with two distinct persons who attempt to blend their individual upbringings into one House brand. That is hard enough. Then they have children, and they attempt to teach their children to adhere to the House brand. And this is where things get even woollier. Children, aside from not emerging from the womb as Christians, are not clones of the husband or wife, or even intersections of their best attributes. They are completely new and unregenerate creations. They have a few borrowed bits here and there, but they're largely themselves. The borrowed bits are not evenly distributed, they are not always the positive bits, and they are not balanced between Dad's Traits and Mum's Traits. They cannot be wholly "like you" unless they grow up in *your* body, household, cultural environments, and formative decade. So we must accept that this is not going to happen, and look at what we have to work with. In the end, a family is rather like a *Masterchef* "Mystery Box," where contestants have to cook up a dish using only what is in the box presented to them.

It is still very tempting to enforce the House brand. But what happens when we have a child who is so completely off-brand that this is not healthy? If you have a family full of intellectuals and they suddenly acquire a child with learning disabilities, you could try to maintain a House brand of "We are brainy, with that little aberration over there." Or, you could redefine the brand: "We are diversely skilled and we help one another."

In a church, we have the same choice. God brings forth new creations in our midst, and we have no say in what their makeup is like. We can either push the House brand at them, creating an exclusion zone, or we can continually expand the House brand to include those whom God has placed there to help shape it. I am not speaking of holiness here—that remains a constant, no matter the brand—but of *flavour*. Look at the people God has gifted you with in your Mystery Box. Incorporate them. Stop wishing you'd been sent *flashier* gifts. Explore their capabilities and let that inform the branding, as it organically morphs with each new addition. Trust the Holy Spirit with them.

God speaks to all of us.

I once watched a video of intercessor Suzette Hattingh conducting a seminar on prayer. She began by asking for prayer topics from the audience. She had these put on the projector and asked everyone in the room to pick an issue with the Holy Spirit to pray about, and have at it. After the prayer session, she surveyed the audience by show of hands to see how many people had picked each topic. She added the statistics onto the projector, and said, "Clearly the Holy Spirit is most concerned here today about this issue," pointing to the largest number, "and next about this," and so on down the list. She had full trust that the Holy Spirit in each person would direct their prayers, and no problem with the prayers being spread out among many topics. That is trusting God to lead people. That is trusting people to let God lead them. That is allowing God to speak *to* the church *through* the church. And that is allowing God to do more than one thing at a time.

The congregation doesn't have to be passive, having agency only in the free worship sessions. It's designed for so much more, and it can't grow past spoon-feeding without some trust being extended to it. Hand it the spoon now and then. *Ask* your congregation what they are puzzled about and need teaching on. *Ask* them what they feel God wants us all to focus on right now. This will be more than one thing;

tackle them Hattingh-style, starting with the highest-frequency topic and working your way down. Ask them what this year's focus should be. Pay attention to the spiritual burdens God places on their hearts, even if they don't seem to match up to the current trend. Don't just nod, train. Don't just train, equip. Don't just equip, release. Don't just release, back them!

The bigger your meeting, the harder it will be to be interactive. So, if we're going to go on having big meetings, we might need to keep on emphasising the importance of smaller meetings, so that we can actually get around to doing 1 Corinthians 14:26. Smaller meetings are really going to shine for those who aren't satisfied with the status quo until the status quo has been allocated a *raison d'être*.

It might be possible to do auditorium meetings as interactive lectures, though, with a roving mike, if you're brave enough to allow questions from the floor. You could allocate a maximum distraction time, say, one minute per question and one minute per answer, and then go back to the main theme. You could have a roving scribe or dedicated SMS line to quietly take questions to be answered in a Q&A after the message, Jesus-style. This would also eliminate early questions that you intend to answer in the course of your message. You could Sermon in the morning meeting and Q&A at the night, or even Q&A once a month with questions coming in all month. Or, after church, you could open your website podcast for comments, though that's risky, because not all enquiries are genuine, not all comments are Biblically supported, and also you could spend the rest of your life answering the mail! These are just ideas to get you thinking on ways to interact with your audience, where they get to say something more than "Amen!" It lets them be more than rows of paper dolls. You won't be thinking of them as paper dolls, but it's cool to find ways to remind them of that.

Not all questions can or should be answered from the pulpit. This is where things come back to relationship, where there are caring one-on-one (or two-on-one) friendships in place to explore difficult, long-term, or sensitive issues.

Caveat: Not everyone wants to interact or have a say. Big, huge grain of pink Himalayan sea salt! There are still a large number of people who just want to be *led.* Some of them want this because they are phlegmatic in nature; some of them are just dead tired from the mental load of the week; and some of them really can't be bothered with doing their own thinking. You'll have to balance the security needs of the first lot with the complacency of the last. I'm not trying to say that the church is looking for leaders who have *no* ideas and rely on us to generate them. The people who just want to be led—they *need* you to bring ideas to the table. All I'm saying is that there should *be* a table, and that more than five people could be sitting at it.

When we have people who come to us with dreams that fall outside our church's scope, how do we encourage autonomy without mutiny? I think it's by being in relationship—neither refusing to have one, nor relegating it to the "Unimportant" box. It's tied to accepting that God speaks to all of us, and that within each person's IEP we'll find things that we didn't anticipate. In other words, we treat adults like adults, and treat Spirit-filled Christians like the Holy Spirit really does live in them and speak to them. We remember that *submission* really means *mutual uplifting,* not restriction or censure or censorship. And we're lovingly honest if we really do sense that the time isn't right for them.

If you have to hold somebody back, please, for the love of God and the love He has for us, do your best to explain why. I understand that some people will not accept any reason, even to the point of being delusional. I understand that the reason itself may be hard to articulate (how on earth do you explain a *squick?*) But consider the alternative. If you don't help someone see *why* they aren't ready, how in the world are they supposed to *get* ready? I still don't know why it happened to me all those years ago. It left me with nothing to work on. I checked with the Holy Spirit. I checked with my husband and friends. I checked my attitude. I checked my lifestyle. I checked my talent. I checked my integrity. I checked my motives. I checked my character, personality, manner, expectations, theology, vision match, submission, dress sense and personal hygiene. I was working hard on all of them, so I came up baffled and wailing Kasey Chambers's "Not Pretty Enough" inside my skull. It would have been a massive relief to know where I was falling down and what I needed to do to *fall up*. I'm sorry to say that the possibility exists that I wasn't *falling* down, I was simply being *kept* down, and that falling up in one area would simply have led to another area being pinpointed. In psychology they call that *unrelenting standards*.

Things are much better now, I'm pleased to say. I have been blessed with a string of fantastic leaders in recent years. They don't see me as a loose cannon, but as a loved contributor. When my pastors talk with me, I get full-body listening. It's so rare and refreshing that I have to stop myself from rambling on just from the sheer wonder of it. (Right now you'll be wishing I had afforded you the same restraint!) I don't get judged, even though my flaws are laid out plain to see. I get encouraged. And I get told the truth. When questions are asked of me, they're not asked out of nosiness or attempts to discredit; they're asked with an end goal in mind of *moving forward together*. There I

Positive conviction *has its roots in a threatless desire to* **please the God I love**, *rather than in* **shame** *that I haven't.*

find correction without blame or threats: positive conviction, that has its roots in a desire to please the God I love, rather than in shame that I haven't. It's coaching without crushing.

When my life group leader talks with me, I get candour. We do life together, so we don't have any "that's easy for you to say" going on. She knows me inside and out, and knows how to call forth the best in me. She also knows how to call out the worst in me, and sometimes she does it without me even feeling ruffled. I think it's because I know she loves me and knows what she's talking about. I can take a rebuke from her fairly easily, because I know she's not looking down her nose at me, but is showing me what I could be, if I pull my head in. It's the difference between "keep up!" and "join me!"

What's special in that friendship is that she's not averse to learning from me in return. My Certificate of Christian Ministry might be 20 years old, but along with a range of authors and pastors, it laid a good theological foundation. I freely acknowledge that I am the sum of the learning that's come my way and the work of God: if He had not brought certain books and sermons and lessons across my path at certain points, I would know nothing. It's not *me* that's bright, it's the authors I've read: and they probably feel the same way about their own writing. My life group leader is a smart, educated woman, yet she loves learning new things and has no problem with them arising from her charges. This kind of teachability is gold. It ensures she will never be caught in the "because I said so" or "we never did it that way before" traps. A leader who "can't be told" anything—either because they think they know it all already, or because they're unsafe to talk to—is at a disadvantage. It is possible to be a receptive person without the river of your orthodoxy necessarily breaking its banks. All that is required is openness and the maintenance of a quiet hotline to the Holy Spirit for checks and balances. None of us are going to earn a tombstone engraved *"Here Lies The Font of All Knowledge"*. All of us will be learning new and wonderful and upcycled things about the Lord until the last possible second on earth ... so long as we wish to! Always encourage your people to be Berean, to explore God and the Word for themselves and not just take your word for it.

I like the idea of having between leadership and laity a mutual learning and respect, as I mentioned last chapter. I like mutual transparency—all of my leaders are people who freely admit they are not God—though I do understand that there are limits, or a limited audience, to the transparency a leader shows. Being "all in this together" is a beautiful thing. It employs humility and accountability. In the past, church members have been required to be the ones who become vulnerable and open up about their lives. Today, we're seeing a lot more reciprocity. Leaders may fear that letting their guard down will lose them respect, but it isn't necessarily so. The leaders I respect most are the ones who are real. They don't live a charmed life, at a remove from the real world, in some place where the grass is greener; and they don't pretend to be angels.

Being all in this together *is a beautiful thing.*

In regard to disclosures, Adrian Plass writes that in some instances walls must remain, for some walls are supporting ones; so knowing your audience is key. I'm just glad my friend didn't create distance between us when she was appointed to a leadership role. And I'm also glad she knows when I'm talking rubbish, because she's the best person to let me know. The days of the ivory tower are thankfully behind the church, and huzzah to that.

How would it be if church staff meetings didn't just include the leaders of each department, but also a randomly selected ground-zero representative from each? Besides demystifying the gathering, it could pay dividends in back-checking the effectiveness of policies. It might smack of trade unionism, but it *is* union we're after, and this could be helpful. Your mileage may vary—you may find that too many cooks in the kitchen spoils the broth—but efforts to make leadership more consultative are going to go over well with your congregation, especially the younger generation. As Patrick Lencioni points out, a lack of debate indicates a lack of trust: people need to weigh in before they can really buy in.

The younger generation, by the way, other than being labelled "entitled", are actually quite nice. Like all people, they just want to be loved, both for their projected selves and their real selves. They need room to grow and freedom to interact. Like light in a vacuum, there's a big part of ourselves that we can only discover and display when we bounce it off others. This is one of the benefits of social media, for all its traps. Don't assume too quickly that social media is shallow and narcissistic, and that its friendships aren't real. It's true that we aim to project only the best parts of ourselves online, but just like face to face conversations, who we really are does leak out. I've made some very deep friendships electronically, and in return gained cross-cultural, cross-generational and cross-denominational insight. The key take-home from the social media frenzy is that *people want to be connected*

People want to be connected and to be seen and heard.

and to be seen and heard. This is a good thing, a thing church can harness and direct into brotherhood, mutual uplift, and peer learning.

I mentioned several chapters back that Generation Z may lack self-sacrifice and community spirit. It's more accurate to say that they like to *define* their own community, and stick to it. I don't see a huge amount of school spirit amongst today's teenagers, but I do see networks of friends. Again this is something directable. It's still a drive toward solidarity, but it retains elements of independence: I can withdraw from this network if I feel threatened, I can eliminate from my circle those who make me feel unsafe, I can control how much I reveal of myself and to whom. These kids do want to belong—but they want to feel safe and retain some autonomy while they do so. Therefore, the way we frame *belonging* in church needs to accommodate that. They may never be flag-wavers and they will never adopt the Pentecostal Two-Step. We'll need to tell them: you belong, but you have freedom, and you're allowed to ask questions—this is not a hivemind. To borrow from the cosmopolis, the church isn't a melting pot, where we all become generic beige blancmange. It's a salad bowl, where we each bring something precious and together produce a community that begs people to taste and see that the Lord is good!

They're not so different from us, are they? And they will employ self-sacrifice in a heartbeat if it's for someone they love. So let's be people and churches they love.

Have a quick look online at generational learning styles and what works for each. If you've ever been in a class which mixed the age groups, you'll have observed that certain styles work best for certain ages. Baby Boomers, for instance, don't appear to like interpretive activities (e.g. r*epresent this feeling as a creature and draw a picture of it*). I noted with amusement at PD sessions that Boomers, if they didn't like or understand the question, would pluck a slightly-more-tolerable question out of thin air, and answer that one instead! Visual Gen X are adventurous and like to circle around a question, seeing it from all sides, preferably with graphs and diagrams. Millennials and Gen Z want to see it represented technologically (because then it's *truly* modern), and interact with it, poking it to see where and what it gives. The lines blur, of course, but it seems to me the older you are, the more you trust data and trust what you're told to believe; the younger you are, the more you need proof and persuasion, and enjoy experimentation.

There's a wealth of delineation on this topic online, which I'll leave you to explore on your own rather than reproducing here. Suffice it to say, if you come up against resistance, try a different teaching tactic. Today's kids may not respond to lecture-style church the way previous generations did or had to. If you see phones being used in your services, it doesn't necessarily mean people are bored and checking social media. Some of us are exploring your points in *Strong's* and *Easton's*, following Holy Spirit-generated rabbit trails, and making notes on the great things you're opening up for us!

> *If you come up against resistance, try a different teaching tactic.*

Lectures, by the way, are less than 5% effective, and even the universities know it. We know that Paul instructed Timothy to preach the Word, just as he did; and we know that Jesus Himself preached. But if God knew that lectures weren't an effective way of imparting information, why would He ask this? When did *preaching* become synonymous with *lecturing*? What else might "preaching" mean? Clearly Paul, whom I imagine as quite an argumentative guy, was a much better writer than speaker.

Another quick dive into *Strong's*: the Hebrew for "preach" is *qara'*, to call out to a person as they pass by (especially by name), to publish, proclaim, even invite. "Preached" is *basar*, to be fresh, to announce, bring, show forth, publish; and *euengelisametha*, to announce good news, declare, bring. "Preacher" is *qoheleth* in Hebrew, an assembler, lecturer. The Greek is *kerusso*, to herald as a public crier, proclaim, publish, especially divine truth. The sense of publish—to bring information to public attention—could relate equally to books as to speech. The famous St Francis quote comes to mind, "and if necessary use words," but ideally words and actions, as per James 2, ought to be working as a duet rather than as rival soloists.

The "call out, especially by name" could be hinting that messages are best delivered in the context of *relational* conversation.

The only reasons I can come up with for God advocating actual lecturing as an impartational tool are:

(1) Even though only 5% of the lecture content will sink in, God knows how to speak between the lines. For each person within earshot, it might be a different 5%. We've all compared notes after sermons and found that our "gold nugget" wasn't the same as our neighbour's. What generally happens for me personally, is that I'll find the gold nugget, and God will use it to take me off on a wild tangent, often dipping back down into the sermon here and there. If you think of it like painting, the preacher is crafting a work of art in, say, blue, but as I follow along, God is whispering, "And add some red just ... there. And oh, look, yellow fits in over here. Now see how the blue works amazingly well."

(2) God will always provide enough "way," like a huge ark only half-filled, even knowing only 5% of what He says will be retained. The truth must be out there to stand witness against those who resist it. Get the word out, even if there is no response. And yet ... no loving parent is satisfied with providing a way for his errant kids to come home, without making a solid effort to chase them down. This would lead us to:

(3) "Go into all the world," meaning, as you are going into the world in all its many spheres, take the breaking news of the Kingdom with you, to reach as many as possible. And here we are given specific tasks: to make disciples and baptise. (Have your parishioners baptised anyone lately?) And there is a vast difference between *church preaching* and *discipling*, though one of course can lead to the other. I submit to you that preaching could be less of a diatribe and more of a dialogue. And if you wouldn't shout at me across a coffee table, don't shout at me across a pulpit.

> *Preaching could be less of a* diatribe *and more of a* dialogue.

Paul preached a magnificent sermon at the Areopagus, but no church in Athens resulted from it. However, the house churches everywhere else, where they all sat around and contributed together in their journey of faith, flourished. Food for thought. Food *with* thought.

If people aren't coming in the doors of the church to our seeker services, maybe the "seekers" should be *us*. Do you want to know what the unchurched do on Sunday mornings? They go to brunch. Sunday is the day they use to catch up with friends and family. It's a day of rest and reconnection. It was always supposed to be. For the churched, on the other hand, Sunday can be a day of frenetic activity, beginning with scrubbing up, dressing up, and showing up (quite early, if you're serving), chivvying the children into the car and drilling them on last week's memory verse; energetic worship, intent listening, crowd mingling—and dropping to the couch when you get home, in order to do it all again in a couple of hours. Don't get me wrong. I adore church and find it invigorating, though I can't always absorb more than one sermon in a day, and I don't see anywhere in the Bible where tabernacle, temple, synagogue or church had even a *once* a week iron requirement. But in no way, shape or form is it a day of rest. The content of the sermon is more likely to be about getting *on* your feet, rather than *off* them.

We have to stop worshipping church. The Bible has a low opinion of Christians who spend all their time and money on the church to the detriment of family members. I'm not saying "don't give and don't go". I'm saying, if the only time we church members have to catch up with our elderly parents, or run around the yard with our kids is Sunday, then we need to make some adjustments. We can either ask God for relief in our work circumstances (perhaps re-prioritising why we work so hard, if that's an issue) or find a church community that isn't Sunday-based. If we tell our families that our time or financial support is "a gift dedicated to God, sometimes by completely destroying it," then according to both Jesus and Paul, we're doing it wrong. The phrase "worse than an unbeliever" is harsh for a reason: people matter. I used to take my family for granted because I saw them as extensions of myself, partakers in my ministry. That was all very well, except that I did not love myself ... and so I failed to love them as myself. Our families, our teams—they must not miss out simply because they're insiders.

If the call of God to ministry trumps every other call on a minister, what does that say about pastors who also hold down an outside job? Only that if the two careers come into conflict, the focus must be on the ministry. So is a "tentmaker" like Paul a minister or a layperson? How do we differentiate between "a call to The Ministry" and "having a ministry"—which should be every one of us? I don't know. Are we all "tentmakers" in the end, due to the inherent priesthood of every believer? Perhaps. I would only say that I totally respect church leaders who have secular jobs because I can always be certain that they speak to me from the ground zero I find myself on. I also think it helps to

> *It helps to be grounded in the community you're trying to reach.*

be grounded in the community you're trying to reach. That said, there are other ways for a leader to transcend the walls of their office—such as volunteering in community projects, helping the town with things that matter *to them*. Each person has to work out with Jesus exactly what He wants from them, whether it be a full-time paid staff position or a mix, and ask Him to help with provision and with focus. I know that sounds glib. But many families in our churches struggle with their careers and the strain one career (or lack of career) puts on the other, and the issues of balancing time versus finance. If this is a situation you, as a leader, are in, it may be a season of opportunity for empathy.

God loves the church passionately, but God is not the church and the church is not God. It's perfectly possible to have a heart sold out to God and His mission, without being run off your feet with God-related paraphernalia. Again, it shouldn't be *God vs. The Things Of God*. Attending church is vitally important, but attending its every event without fail is not. I had one youth leader tell me lovingly at 22, working full time, that I needed to give up ten of my sixteen commitments because "God doesn't get a whole lot of glory out of frazzled Christians." She was right. I grew up living a purpose-driven life; it had never occurred to me to live a loved-driven, sustainable one. I'd been thinking I needed an alibi in order to justify a "no". There was an even deeper truth at play, too: God isn't about driving you into the ground. He requires sacrifice, yes, but it is the loving sacrifice of a family member, not the cannon-fodder sacrifice of a pawn.

And For My Next Trick ...

I'm thinking about asking a local café if, every so often, I can just sit down at a table of a Sunday morning, with a smile and a sign saying "All Genuine Questions About God Attempted," and see what happens. ("Genuine" would be a stipulation because it *can* be a waste of time to argue over "old chestnuts" with people who are only heckling. "Attempted" would be my disclaimer to being the Font of All Knowledge. In the end, all of us are only attempting our answers anyway, so hopefully this would also introduce a note of camaraderie.)

I don't have the wherewithal to hire a master chef and open my own café and name it *Questions*. You can, if you like—I could do the branding for you—but if you do, make sure you feed body, soul and spirit well! Be explorative, not defensive, and serve amazing coffee.

In a local watering hole I'll learn something from anyone who poses searching questions. Sometimes it reveals their individual stumbling-block, or the spiritual *location* of their "God-shaped hole." At the very least, perhaps I'll get to know someone and become the friend they catch up with on Sundays.

Talk to the Lord. Find out what *He* would like to see change. Listen honestly and, if you can, without confirmation bias. Ask Him for strategies to lead each subsequent generation like the sons of Issachar, understanding the times.

11 An Ounce of Prevention

NOBODY SETS OUT TO HAVE awful things happen in their church. How can we prevent them? How can we handle them? What can we learn from them?

Communication is your friend here. If you permit—encourage—people to talk about what's bothering them in the hierarchy, yes, you'll have to field a lot of vitriol. But you'll also catch the little foxes before they chomp down the whole vineyard. Foxes, as it happens, are in the canine family, and grapes are toxic to dogs: you're doing the foxes a favour as well as the vineyard. Be available, listen, correct, or go in to bat as needed. At the very least, you'll be able to clear up misunderstandings that have arisen from assumptions. Many times when we are hurt, it turns out to not be a matter of thoughtless indifference or malice, but an accident, a misunderstanding, or a miscommunication.

In every interpersonal conflict scenario, we have to decide which is most important: the issue at stake, the wellbeing of the person we're in conflict with, our own wellbeing and/or pride, or the relationship between us. There are times when each of these may genuinely be the priority. In an ideal world, these four things would not be in competition; but I find it useful and calming to use this system to sift through what I'm feeling and get to the core of what matters. Getting all four things aligned is an apex skill I aspire to.

The *issue* comes first if it is a moral issue—if one of you is causing harm to another, or engaging in unrepented sin. The *other's wellbeing* comes first if they have simply slipped up and need forgiveness (as opposed to a pattern) or if they are impaired in some way and can't help it; in which case love covers a multitude of sins. *Your wellbeing* comes first if you are consistently being treated as though you don't matter; this is distinct from "my pride is injured".

The *relationship* comes first if we are dedicated to keeping doors of love open—if the relationship is worth keeping, despite the need for regular tune-ups. In pastoral ministry, this becomes especially important. When I'm disagreeing with a leader, what I desperately want is to hear something like, "I may not agree with what you're saying/doing, I may not be able to let it continue unchallenged, but I will always love you and believe in you." Psychologist Dr Gavin Brown says, "In all of our relationships, we are always asking two basic questions: *am I safe*, and *will you be there for me?*"

When is each thing not the priority? The *issue* is not the priority if it's a non-essential thing and it's become a relational obstacle, such as the vegetarian not tolerating the steak-lover. The *other's wellbeing* comes second if they are being abusive toward you. *Your wellbeing* comes second if God is asking you to lay it aside temporarily for your brother. And *the relationship* can no longer be paramount if it's consistently destructive, or has reached the threshold where disfellowshipping is the only Biblical response.

If abuse has found a foothold in a gap you can close, consider policy changes to close that gap, rather than making exceptions to a rule that goes on gaping. Evaluate whether the methods of the past are still serving you all well, or whether they need updating. It's a good idea, though not pleasant, to familiarise yourself with the grooming tactics used by predators, and nip any of those possibilities in the bud. Have a spiritual abuse policy, the same way most organisations have policies around disclosures of other types of abuse. Never think "it couldn't happen in my church." Do all you can to make it *freakishly difficult* for it to happen in your church.

> *Never think "it couldn't happen"; make it freakishly difficult for it to happen.*

When employing people, ensure you don't place the gift before the character. This might seem counter to what I said about letting imperfect people use their gifts. Leadership is a gift that messes with the lives of others. Remember that in many church government models, staff are not *voted* into office, but picked or hired by the top people. This means that the lives being messed with have *no say in who* is messing with them. Their choice is to like it, lump it, or leave. If, as a church member, you've removed yourself from a department because the leadership was untenable, it can be quite demoralising to sit in the congregation, knowing you could make a worthwhile contribution if you'd only be willing to sacrifice your sanity/dignity/family ... while the pastor continues to preach about not burying your talent, stepping out of the boat, and so on.

Know your employees. Know the things they need to work on, know their strengths, pay attention to who they are when they think you're not watching. Understand where they best fit. In government, it often seems to me that MPs are handed portfolios almost at random, whether they are passionate about those fields or not. I am confident we can do better than that, when it comes to fitting square pegs to square holes.

An Ounce of Prevention

Protect your people from your employees. Make sure you are a *safe* person to tell hard things to. Give your people permission to speak honestly and respectfully to you, even if negative things have to be brought up. There's a difference between a negative conversation and a necessary one: make sure you are not invoking the No Talk Rule. People shouldn't have to don the full armour of God just to survive the conversation. There's no point having an open door policy if what waits inside the open door is a great big boot. Be someone safe to confide in, both in terms of confidentiality and in terms of your reactions (staunchness, disbelief, disgust, horror, denial, anger) and the possible fallout for the person who is bravely putting up their hand.

Make sure you are a safe person *to tell* hard things *to.*

Whistle-blower retribution absolutely happens in church: it's the squeaky wheel that gets the grease. Ensure your people are not left without recourse. The scary leader might well be like a son or daughter to you. That doesn't mean you are off the hook when it comes to being a father or mother to everyone else. Understand that a member may well follow the Scriptural method for dispute resolution, but it doesn't guarantee them a golden outcome. It just means they obeyed Scripture and operated righteously. A member can take their problem directly to the staff member responsible, and get shredded. It has to be feasible for them to take the next steps, assuming they're still breathing. Be there for them.

When someone comes to you and discloses spiritual abuse, take them seriously. Let their voices be heard—not silenced, or swept under the rug, or waited out. Talk to the victim frankly and compassionately. Listen. Listen hard. Get the facts without victim-blaming (remember the rape analogy). Talk to the alleged perpetrator separately and get their side of the story. Talk to witnesses, if there are any. Don't sit on the evidence and wait for things to die down, hoping it will all go away. That will just give the abuser carte blanche. If it's a criminal matter, of course you must report it fully and immediately and halt it in its tracks, though you won't *necessarily* broadcast the matter to the whole church. But spiritual abuse is slipperier, and comes more under the heading of "things we don't go to law over in front of unbelievers."

By all means counsel the abuser and, if they respond well (restitution is a good start) and depending on what they did, maybe afford them a second chance. Avoid giving them a fifth and sixth chance if there is a trail of injured people continuing to hobble out the door. It will look to those wounded souls like *jobs for the boys* and reinforce to them that *some animals are more equal than others.* It's a hard, hard call when you love all the people involved. Do not under any circumstances move them on unchecked, undisciplined, unmonitored or unrepentant to some other church, to start abusing a fresh bunch of people. They must attend somewhere, sure; but they must not be given authority without rehabilitation.

Once the bull has left the china shop, it's possible to cut someone's recovery time in half, if you only humble yourself and apologise for any part you played in what happened to them. It doesn't mean you necessarily *sinned;* it just means you were the responsible officer when

> *Simply* saying sorry
> *can cut someone's grief in half.*

disaster struck on your watch. Engage your empathy. It can become a choice between your pride and their wellbeing. You want them to get better, right? So if you *can* take this step, know that it can make a world of difference.

If you *don't* feel at all responsible, well, we even say "I'm sorry" when a person is bereaved, and it doesn't mean we *caused* that death, just that we are sorrowed at how it affects the person. Let them know that at the very least, you share in their sorrow. And if you are at fault in the situation, admit where. These are the things that make us give undying love to a leader: when they are not too proud to be human, when they identify with us, when they can admit their limitations, when they prove that at heart they just want us to thrive in God.

> Grace *goes with* truth
> Righteousness *goes with* peace
> Justice *goes with* mercy

I've recently been re-introduced to the subject of *restitution*. I don't believe I've ever heard a single sermon on this subject. Maybe we are afraid that restitution sits in conflict with grace (because it smacks of earning) and forgiveness (because it smacks of addressing debt). It is, however, a Biblical concept that does a work of goodness in the hearts of both the hurter and the hurtee. I confess I am not too well-studied on this topic, but there is precedent in both Testaments for it: the Levitical requirement to compensate fourfold for damages, and the example of Zacchaeus, in whom it arose as a spontaneous response to salvation.

Even restitution, when proffered by a repentant leader, cannot turn back the clock. But as I've said, even a simple unbending to apologise can go a long way. A present goes even further. I'm not sure what an appropriate restitution for spiritual abuse would look like. I'm not talking about money. In the world, they sue, and restitution is a financial affair. I don't know that that would hit the spot. A more personal, caring response would be a better fit. It would probably need to be something tailored to the specific situation. You may merely need to spend six months humbly listening to them process it until it's out of their system. Or you may need a grand gesture. If you're in a traumatic church where people caught in sin are made to confess it from the platform ... will *you* likewise confess your handling errors? We must at the very least acknowledge privately that things went down, even if such an admission carries legal fears. I don't mean to be harsh, but honestly, this healthy fear serves a leader better at the *front* end of the situation, not the retrospective!

When you have the initial choice about how to handle someone, it can't hurt to ask yourself: if you weren't protected by the idea that Christians ought not to sue one another over moral failings, would this be grounds for a lawsuit? It's a question that would help us do *better* than the world. Grace and truth go hand in hand. Righteousness and peace kiss each other: you can't ask a person for peace if you're enabling unrighteousness that impacts on them. Justice and mercy must go together. We can't simply ask people to forgive, and fail to address the problems that gave rise to the situation.

Rachel Denhollander talks without rancor about these issues in some depth when she says,

> *"When those verses [about God bringing goodness out of evil] are interpreted properly they are glorious and beautiful truths. More often than not, particularly in the case of sexual*

> *The key thing is to demonstrate that restoring relationship is a priority.*

> *assault, they're really used to mitigate and to minimize—almost as if the victim handles it 'properly,' if the victim just forgives, all of the feelings are going to go away. That's not true and that's not what Scripture teaches. ... Church is one the least safe places to acknowledge abuse."*

Having acknowledged any fault, repented if necessary, and asked forgiveness, the key thing in restitution is to demonstrate proactively that *restoring loving relationship* with that person is a priority. One of the most damaging things that happened to me in my case, was that when I recognised that I needed counselling to begin to heal, the church charged me for it. It felt rather like being hit by a car and then sent the panelbeating bill. It was exactly the reverse of restitution. I'm happy to say that this policy is no longer in play, and upon later enquiry turned out to be a case of misdirection. When I finally forgave, I released all debts and expectations of recompense, so that *I* could walk free. I'm just exploring better handling techniques. We're always about doing better next time. I do believe that leaders, on the whole, very much want their people to thrive in God. I believe they love us, usually more than we can casually observe. It's why I choose to trust again.

When should you not counsel someone? When their issues are above your paygrade. When they are outside your purview. When you're not qualified.

The tendency in church life is to tackle *everything* from the theological end. While this is good from the "letting God handle it" point of view, it can leave large gaps, not because God is inadequate but because ordination training is. A person like me can get caught in the middle, when we have *psychological* issues but believe we are broken because the incoming *spiritual* answers aren't doing the trick.

You can't just tell people to "take every thought captive" and not show them that this passage is specifically dealing with spiritual warfare. Without that context, this verse does seem to imply that *every passing thought* ought to be swiped into a butterfly net, pounded with a rock until it conforms, and then put neatly on the correct shelf with a solid "Hmph!" You'll have people trying to catch all the random things that flit through the brain second by second simply because that's how the brain works. You'll trap them in hyper-alert guilt for having a human body, in other words. Instead, let them know that if there's a stronghold at play, thoughts *relative to that stronghold* need to be addressed in case they are lies. For example, the lie "The love of God is not for you, you are too far gone" needs to be arrested, tried and found guilty of lying. It is a pretension, claiming that your sin is bigger than the love of God. It must be demolished, but sometimes it is built on a foundation of bitter roots that have to be explored and exposed first. Remember, the passage starts out by saying that these things have to be fought with *spiritual weapons for demolishing strongholds*. God doesn't expect you to defeat them armed with nothing but positive thinking and Prozac.

Also, don't quote "As a man thinks in his heart, so is he." That is a remarkably poor translation of Proverbs 23:7 that occurs only in the King James Version. The word given "thinks" means *reckoned* or *calculated*. The context of the passage is *hospitality*, not mental hygiene:

> *"...for he is the kind of person who is always thinking about the cost. "Eat and drink," he says to you, but his heart is not with you."* (NIV)

It warns that a host who counts the dollar value of your every mouthful at his party, is likely to try to get dollar for dollar at yours—so don't eat more than you can cater for in return! And, possibly, that any covenant with such a person is a bad idea, since they are focussed on economics, not relationship.

This verse has been used for centuries to make Christians believe that *they are their bad thoughts*. Not so. Bad thoughts, good thoughts, indifferent thoughts—they are all randomly generated by the brain all day. You don't have to pick a fight with each one. Just refocus: think about that which is pure, lovely, of good report, excellent, praiseworthy ... think about Jesus, who is Himself all of these things. If the definition of *repent* is *to do a u-turn*, to about-face and walk away, to rise back up to the heavenly vantage point, then that's what you're doing when you redirect yourself to Him.

As I've mentioned, God is thrifty and will use even a mistranslation to bring us closer to Him. If you've gotten good mileage in your life out of "As a man thinks, so he is," then kudos to you. There is indeed a sense that our thinking habits will give shape to our lives. But now that you know the Proverb is not about cognition, don't continue to teach from it as though it were. Some of the things in my life were taught to me correctly, and I distorted them as I listened. Other things were taught out of balance with other things—as human trends and God-engineered emphases came and went in the church. And occasionally things were taught that were just flat-out wrong. It's a great idea to do a word and

---

People who have suffered serious trauma *need to be referred to those* best equipped *to move them forward.* It may not be you.

An Ounce of Prevention

idiom study in several translations (and the original language) to be sure that what you're teaching is the real deal.

Theology alone is not enough for people who have suffered serious trauma and abuse in their life. They need to be referred to those best equipped to move them forward. It may not be you, despite your hotline to the Throne and your immense concern for them. This kind of thing requires specialised training. Give them what you do have—pastoral care, prayer support, prophetic insight—but also send them to someone who knows what you do not know. If you don't have a degree in psychology, refer them to someone in the community who does. In fact, go out of your way to build relationship with that someone—not so you can discuss your congregant, of course, but so you can offer a spectrum of care as colleagues. You won't be privy to the case work, but you can still complement it by offering loving and wise spiritual support while the person unravels their cognitive stuff with the psychologist.

Psychology is not the enemy of faith. Each has its limits. Shouting verses at yourself will not heal you if they are guesswork verses conjured up by a third party. Behaviour modification will not move you forward if there are bitter spiritual roots poisoning your soul. But together, ministry and psychology can be the right and left hands of God, mending and sculpting as He makes something beautiful out of our lives. So, if we're going to partner with psychologists in practice, why not also partner with them in respectful relationship? Perhaps the time will come when that professional will refer to *you* any clients asking spiritual questions.

I recommend all pastoral counsellors undertake prayer ministry training. The help I've received from trained prayer ministers has enabled God to turn my life around. I'd like to see every believer get the same help, actually, because we all have *stuff*.

A word about dealing with women. If you are a male leader, try to remember that women comprise fully half of the adults in your congregation. They are not a minority or a side project. And many of them have struggled to find an interstice between *abject* and *object* in which to move. We need to hold that door wide open. There is a perception among some male leaders that women habitually exaggerate their feelings ("because they couldn't *possibly* feel things that deeply"). There is a tendency among a few female leaders to emulate *male* leaders and encourage other women to do likewise. Both of these attitudes come at women from a "man up!" stance.

Women are not designed to man up.

But here's the thing: women are not designed to *man up*. For one thing, our biology is routinely leaning all over our inner self fully 50% of the time, with a special amount of ferocity for the final few days. This is not a fault or an excuse: it is our design. When you ask a woman to man up, you're asking her to deviate from her blueprint and be something other than what God made her. It's not that women have less emotional self-control than men—just that we have to work harder for it. Or, perhaps, that the wobbliest of our boundaries tends toward the tearful, where a man's might tend toward the angry. I'm making huge generalisations here, so please take this with a pinch of grace. I am not saying all women are blubberers and all men are temperamental. We could make a case that when it comes to self-mastery, testosterone provides an equal level of challenge to be overcome as does estrogen. I am simply relating what it feels like to have to push past your biology in order to function professionally. 50% of the time, it feels like the wheels are constantly in danger of coming off. Since we can't let this happen, we become hypervigilant, which increases our stress load. We can ask the

Lord for relief from the symptoms of PMS. We can ask Him to breathe through us His patience and kindness and self control. But we cannot, and should not, stop being women.

Whatever the case, please never ask a woman to be man-like. That's as leaden a balloon as when men are asked to sing what they call "Jesus is my boyfriend" choruses. And on the soul/spirit level, biology aside, asking a woman to *man up* is asking her to stop manifesting the side of God's image which He Himself has described at times as a mother hen, or a nursing mother. God made man in His image, but He also made woman in His image. There are things unique to womanhood which show forth the nature of God in ways that manhood does not. To absent them is to lose part of the revelation of who God is.

At the other end of the spectrum is when women are asked not to *man up*, but to *woman down*. It sounds like this: "Why are you still pursuing ministry opportunities? You've got a baby now." I guarantee you, no new *father* has had this pushed at him! It is a sexist message sent exclusively to new mothers, and it has no place in the twenty-first century.

When my husband Chris and I had our first child, we were leading one of the congregational worship teams. I took two weeks off. I flagged a little more when we had our second (the first being the type to run laps of the auditorium). I tried to make it a short break, but the church structure changed and there was no crèche service for under twos, while Chris's shift work was constant; so I was forced to sit out for two years. It's hard, listening to "get off the bench and into the game" sermons, whilst *chained* to the bench by circumstance. I got back in at the earliest opportunity, but it involved demotion, despite initial promises to the contrary, and this is when the period of spiritual abuse took place. The hardest thing I had to forgive was that I cannot give my children back their early childhood with an *undamaged* mother. I also cannot regret serving God to the best of my ability in each season of my life, though no doubt the "family is also ministry" balance was not always right. The best I can do is ask my children's forgiveness for the past, and be the mother they need today.

Now, this hammering on the door of service with a toddler under each arm isn't everyone's path. You might find it's more sensible to compartmentalise life into *exclusive* seasons. But I had come from a purpose-driven upbringing, in which taking a break was close to apostasy, and serving God was a family affair. I saw no reason why giving birth should cause me to dump the call of God on my life, when He Himself was suggesting no such thing to my heart. I wanted my children to grow up seeing *serving in God's House* as the rule, not the exception. So we brought our kidlets to rehearsals and to the service, where kind friends would hold them while we did our thing on the platform. When my husband was working shifts, I carried the can. At one point I even made them their own tiny team shirts.

It would be fair to point out that while I was busy doing the songleading, it meant that someone else had to be doing the mothering. But it would be equally fair for me to point out that a huge proportion of modern women are building their careers and family nest eggs on the back of childcare services, to the tune of up to 40 hours a week. For me to ask for half an hour of a Sunday, in order to build the Kingdom, is a much smaller ask for a much greater cause. I had dreams of songleading with the baby on my hip, but whilst this is a charming and inclusive (if rather hippie-like) picture, the reality is that the baby *will* keep grabbing at your hair, mike, and earrings, wriggling and babbling (to say nothing of reaching for lunch!) You do end up having to enlist an extra pair of arms, so you can minister effectively and hands-free. And as I said, nobody baulks when a *man* hands over the baby to serve; so according to Galatians 3:28, nobody should baulk when a woman does it.

Looking back, it would have been better for the kids if Chris and I had split ourselves across two teams, instead of rostering and

> *I did not invite my kids into my ministry;
> I assumed. This was a mistake.*

carpooling together. Then only one of us would have needed to be two hours early, making Sundays much less of an ordeal for the children, and needing nobody else to babysit them while we were "working". And honesty compels me to admit that trying to make my children part of the team didn't really work for them. It didn't occur to me, when they were very young, to *ask* or *invite* them into it. I took it for granted that what God called *me* to do, they were bound to do alongside me. My husband and I had many conversations about what constituted a healthy level of church involvement, but I never had this conversation with the kids, as I felt it was *our* decision. This was a mistake. And so my kids grew up seeing that church involvement was not optional—and largely disliking it. As of this writing, my children are reconfiguring what they believe. It's necessary, and I know God's got things in hand, but it's hard to watch. The take-home here is that you can lead a horse to water—the very best water—and you can normalise the drinking of it, but you can't make them drink, at least not indefinitely. They will take ownership of their faith when they can choose to hold and express it according to their own IEP. All of us have to individuate at some point, and this is the point we're in at the moment as a family.

For my own self, God had to teach me that my level of involvement didn't affect how He felt about me, because an *I-am-loved*-driven life trumps a purpose-driven life, and He wants my heart more than He wants my energy. To this day, I have to watch that I don't talk more *about* God than *to* Him, lest He observe at the end, "But I never *knew* you."

An Ounce of Prevention

Talk to God. Ask Him to reveal gaps that need closing, hearts that need mending, and the right counsel (or referral) in each case. Ask Him to help you temper truth with grace, justice with mercy, and righteousness with peace. Stay close to His heart, and behold it regularly.

12 Sharing Shoes

IT SOUNDS GROSS, DOESN'T IT? Washing feet muddied by sweat, dust, and donkey dirt probably isn't much fun either. But the great thing about leadership done well is that not only does the leader learn to walk a mile in the church member's moccasins, but the member learns to step up onto the leader's stilts, too, and get a wider vision.

The best leaders are willing to walk the long walk with their people. As I said in the little bit about visiting preachers, local pastors are invested for the long haul. That doesn't mean they can't move on when God calls; it just means that they operate at all times with the view that they're going to be around to see the fruit of their labours. They are therefore very conscious of their responsibility, and quite protective. A visiting evangelist can say what he likes—he won't be there if it all falls down later. He also has the luxury of living full time in the Big Picture. A careful pastor, mindful of the small pictures and the long haul, is selective about who can and who can't speak into her people's lives.

People don't change overnight. They might experience transformation—such as the drug addict who is spontaneously delivered—but even that person has to grow in Christ if they are to not fall back into the same rut that got them into drugs in the first place. It can be hard work to walk with a person who is slow to change. It can be frustrating when your advice is not heeded or not sinking in. All of this is human, and you'd be less than human if you didn't feel it now and then. In those moments, draw on the strength of Jesus. He is not frustrated, nor impatient. He is writing the person's IEP and He knows exactly what it's going to take to get them home. You get to go along for the ride and be part of the solution.

Leadership is a motivational gift. I think that means it's built in, God-guided, rather than something that comes upon you at salvation or the baptism of the Holy Spirit. Leadership is not itself a fruit of the Spirit. Incidentally, the *fruit* of the Spirit is singular (not *fruits*). And what grows in us (all too gradually) is the manifold flavour of God Himself. Not to put impossible expectations on you, but as time goes by, your leadership should become more and more redolent of love, joy, peace, patience, kindness, goodness, gentleness/humility/meekness, faith-filled-ness/faithfulness, and self-control. Probably all of us have worked under leaders who were lacking one or two of these flavour nuances. Probably all of them were working on them, though, as we all are.

> *God is* incredibly kind, *and* He's *the One you're emulating.*

Kindness is an underrated flavour. I've seen leaders who were smart but scornful, talented but dismissive, in high positions but ungracious. This won't be you. God is incredibly kind, and He's the one you're emulating. I talked in Chapter 8 about my paranoia that *stretching* would turn out to mean *the rack*. But when I look back over my life, except for the times I've been caught in the backwash of other people's mistakes, I see that God has always led me gently. He has even been so kind as to teach me things through methods I've found stimulating and relaxing. For instance, I knew from a previous prophecy that God was going to teach me, for my future ministry, about doing small things well. What I didn't expect was that He would do so by getting me interested in craft, of all things. I had expected some sort of drudgery, but instead I was blessed with a hobby that enriches my life to this day.

You might dream of being dynamic, charismatic and powerful, but you might achieve that through the simple means of dealing kindly with the people around you. It's the soft seawater that wears away the sharp edges of stones. Our unobtrusive qualities can have an unexpectedly greater effect than our obvious ones, as the pen is mightier than the sword, or as the patient, self-controlled man is better than the conqueror. Our own soul is harder to bring to heel than a city.

Heroes come in all stripes, but I've learned to be cautious about swooning over them. All of them, without exception, have feet of clay, and so do I. These days I try to laud the good in them, and be merciful about the not-so-good. A hero is someone to walk behind, but also someone to walk beside, if they'll let you. I try to hold my esteem of them lightly. From pastors to politicians, I'll salute the uniform, but I'll believe in the person. At times it will be and/or.

Speaking of soldiers ... this might sound controversial, and in no way do I intend any disrespect to those who feel strongly the other way. Here it is: while you might be a soldier of Jesus Christ, I'm not fully convinced that the average Christian is. Paul uses military language sparingly. Only four people, and by implication a fifth, are referred to as soldiers: the Messiah, the apostle, the aide, and two pastors. None of these people were laymen. Nowhere in Scripture is the Church referred to as, or compared to, an army. "My great army that I sent among you" referred to the *enemies* of Israel. Songs about marching to battle are from the reigns of David and his successors, when they actually *did* march into battle.

The church at Ephesus, sitting in the stronghold of the cult of Artemis, is instructed to corporately don the whole armour of God, as they are embroiled in a specific spiritual battle. According to Clinton E. Arnold, the full armour of God is for putting on one another—guarding and equipping one another in Christ to resist evil together—rather than something we put only on ourselves, and in isolation. The other two mentions of armour are in Romans 13, where we are told to put on the armour *[instruments, tools, weapons]* of light and clothe ourselves with Christ; and Paul's description of himself and his co-workers (again, not laity) as those wearing armour or wielding weapons of righteousness in both hands. The rest of the quantum leap into seeing the Body as an army might owe its origins more to Christendom than to the Word. I'm not quite educated enough to be sure; but I feel there's room for debate about how widely "army" can be applied to the whole church or to individual Christians. I see the "soldier" role, therefore, as possibly more like elite peacekeeping troops, rather than Everyman. You can have a drink with the soldier, and thank him for what he does to keep you safe, but you aren't trained to do his job, and nor do you want it. I could be wrong, of course; but there's wiggle room, and where there's wiggle room, it's best not to be too dogmatic. If we're going to preach from 2 Timothy on Soldier = Army, we should probably be equally preaching Athlete = Olympic Team and Farmer = Co-op.

Where there's wiggle room it's best not to be too dogmatic.

Sharing Shoes

Please try to be mindful of this if you're going down the "church should be a boot camp" road, or if you have visions of being a drill sergeant with an obedient corps. If we don't see Jesus barking out, "Drop and give me twenty, Maggot," then it's best we don't operate that way either! Jesus specifically contrasted His expectations of the disciples' leadership style, with the way the Romans lorded it over those under them. Interestingly, He didn't say, "Here's what the Roman army does, but here's what *your* army does." Instead, He went directly past all question of armies or governments, to the root issues of ambition and prestige, and undercut those.

I've seen a lot of emphasis on discipline, over the years. There's value in it, but it's not the only value. I haven't heard a lot of sermons about things on the other end of the scale, like *the Sabbath rest of God*. Maybe that emphasis will have its turn again sometime in the future. Me, I can't approach my relationship with God via military discipline, any more than I can run my marriage that way. It's too cold and formulaic and duty-ish for me. He's more than a box I tick off on my *To Do* list. Making time and denying the self—those things I can do, without encasing them in rigidity, reducing them to formality, filling out forms or using a punch-clock. And however obedient I might be to my pastors, however willing to "suck it up, Marine" now and then, I certainly don't want to address them—people who love and care for me—with "Sir, yes, sir!"

On the other hand ... the beauty in the military is that they are, in the end, people who would seriously die for one another, and they sign on in that knowledge. So if we're going to preach militarism, the sacrificial element has to be spoken of as going both ways—otherwise we're asking for a level of dedication that we aren't exemplifying. I can't deny that we do find ourselves in spiritual battles, and that discipline and training are good for that. It's only problematic when we start to treat others as though their day-to-day concerns are beneath a Christian. It was Timothy, one specific pastor, who was asked to stay above civilian affairs (who knows, perhaps he was drowning in them?). We're not to *worry* about our affairs, but we *are* to go about our business—to go into all the world. We're back at the Big Picture vs Smaller Picture again, aren't we? We are living in war times, but we must needs concentrate also on the life at hand, and live that well.

Don't get into empire building, even if the empire you dream of is a godly one. The *Kingdom* is not the same thing as an *empire*. Nowhere are we told to go out and conquer the world, or bend it to a shape. What we are told to do is to go into all the world and make disciples. It's a grassroots movement with its focus on the heart. Every time we try to empirise it, trouble results: power corrupts, persecution of dissenters ensues, it gets co-opted by fiscal and military and political agendas, wars break out. Even on a small scale, this happens. If Jesus had intended us to build an empire, He likely would have demonstrated it by overthrowing Tiberius and naming Himself Caesar. The modern western world, in the "ungodliness" stakes, gives Ancient Rome a run for its money, and vice versa. Yet to those living in the heart of the conquering empire, Paul wrote that the church should see itself as "*more* than conquerors." The weapons of our warfare are not earthly. Our world is occupied by the forces of self-interest. And He says to us, not "change *that*," but "help Me change *them*." And this is what He demonstrated. He made disciples, and He went around doing good and healing people from the devil's influence. He said the Kingdom of God was within us. It is a rock that grows to become a mountain that fills the earth, but it is not a rock cut out by human hands.

Make no mistake, I believe in social justice. I applaud those who bring necessary change, and who stand up for what is right. I believe that our nations are better served when those in power have bowed the knee to Christ. We need righteous laws. The oppressed need relief. But for all of that, I don't believe that seeking clout and pushing godliness

> *Pushing godliness down from above is not a substitute for discipling alongside.*

down from the top, is the same thing as making disciples, which is more of an "alongside" activity. So, while I grew up with a big push to "get a vision, get out there and change the world for Christ," I notice that the Word checks my delusions of grandeur not once, but twice. It says,

> *I urge, then, first of all, that petitions, prayers, intercession and thanksgiving be made for all people - for kings and all those in authority, that we may live peaceful and quiet lives in all godliness and holiness. This is good, and pleases God our Saviour, who wants all people to be saved and to come to a knowledge of the truth. (1 Timothy 2:1-4)*

> *And in fact, you do love all of God's family throughout Macedonia. Yet we urge you, brothers and sisters, to do so more and more, and to make it your ambition to lead a quiet life: you should mind your own business and work with your hands, just as we told you, so that your daily life may win the respect of outsiders and so that you will not be dependent on anybody. (1 Thessalonians 4:10-12)*

It implies that the best way to win souls is to love the brethren, live in holiness, and have a good work ethic. You can do this in your backyard and you can do it in the wilds or ghettoes of the mission field. Were there special circumstances in Ephesus and Thessaloniki that required a clean nose rather than a lobby group? Probably. Many injustices ran unchecked, in addition to a culture of idolatry. But the people leading these practices—people like Caligula!—were to be prayed for, rather than overthrown. We're asked to operate differently from the world. We're to honour, not revile, even when it makes little sense on the surface. We're asked to love the sinner while hating the sin. So while evil empires do rise, they get their comeuppance from God, not from us. If God directs you to run for office, then more power to you—but do so from under Jesus's yoke. Recognise that your job will have its limitations and that it isn't the path for all of us. Recognise also that at times God will ask an individual to vote one way, and other individual to vote another way. It could be about obedience, and therefore a work in their heart as they vote outside their comfort zone. It could be about specific numbers in the results for specific parties or candidates. Remember, He's the God of the Neros as well as the Augustines, the Nebuchadnezzars and the Cyruses. He has His reasons.

You might have a big dream to build an empire in your town: the best services with the best music, the best youth ministry, the best community programs, the best this, the best that. Hold the phone. Unless this is something God has birthed in your heart, and you're sure of that, stop and breathe for a minute. Have you done a demographic survey of this town? Have you researched its history, and the influences and events that have shaped it? What are its key needs and dreams? What are the other ministries already operating in the neighbourhood? Have you consider *partnership?*

I'm an idealist, so bear with me as I float my utopic ideas for your consideration. I have a dream. I dream that the churches in a given area have a loving and functional fraternal network. I dream that they care about each other. I dream that they divvy up the needs of the town according to the gifts given each fellowship. You've got one church just packed with bands: let the other churches support them wholeheartedly as they run the outreach events. You've got one church with a missionary out on the field—give them your missions offering! You've got one church burning to serve the needs of the poor and marginalised: equip them to do so, funding their charity drives! You've got one church with a trained counselling centre—send your troubled people to talk with them. You've got one church with a huge hall—let that be the venue for conferences. Share the load. Share the responsibilities. Share the laughter and tears. Work together across the spectrum of needs in that town, instead of setting up a dozen small duplicates. If one church has a fantastic youth ministry, you don't need five more ineffective ones to service that town, unless there is a real point of difference. You just need to love and support one another. That will be a draw card as well as common sense.

Perhaps this is a good time to bring up projects. I've been talking all along about leading a people, that is, a congregation of some sort, with consultation and feedback and mutuality. Things are going to look quite different if we talk about leading a project strikeforce of some sort for a specific mission, e.g. setting up a crisis response shelter. When you're executing a short-term strategic plan, there's less room for role ambiguity and mucking around. That's not the same thing as doing life, which takes a great deal longer. There's a good deal less politeness in a SWAT team on the scene, and communication doesn't run to "checking in with you" or "brainstorming." Also, planning is clear-cut at the outset and, as far as possible, people stick to the plan and to their roles. In those cases, my hippie ideals of what leadership

You can't run a congregation *like a SWAT team any more than you can run a* SWAT team *like a congregation.*

could be can go out the window. Of course people's domestic concerns sound like First World Problems. You still love and respect the people working with you, but your focus is sharper, and so is your tongue. Let me emphasise that the reverse also holds true: it's not advisable to run a congregation like a SWAT team, any more than you can run a SWAT team like a congregation. But your SWAT team knows you'll take a bullet for them, so they'll excuse a little incidental gruffness.

If you are a church member and you're reading this because you'd like to be a better support to your leaders, let me direct your attention to Galatians 6:6: "The one who receives instruction in the Word should share all good things with their instructor." The text doesn't draw a line between "all good spiritual insights" and "all good any-kind-of-things." The context is around sharing each other's burdens and the law of sowing and reaping. I believe that means that the congregation must not thanklessly milk the pastoral family. We are to share their burdens – whether they be moral support, financial or practical burdens. Possibly, he's reminding them of what he told the Corinthians: that those who dedicate their lives to preaching are entitled, says God, to earn a living from it. Maybe the Galatians hadn't yet taken the hint.

> *Never pass up a* chance to be a blessing.

When Paul says "a man reaps what he sows," he may mean, "The pastor has sown into you, and God will have him reap blessings either through you or in spite of you, so why not come on board and be part of it?" Or, he may mean, "If you sow stinginess, indifference or thoughtlessness toward your pastor, then that will eventually be what

Sharing Shoes

you experience in life." I mention this not as a warning (though it is one!) but as an opportunity. Think about it. If the pastor is showering us with support, and we are likewise showering him with support, is that not a beautiful picture of Christianity? Is that not one of our goals: to outdo one another in expressions of love? Wouldn't the most fun argument of all be the one that went, "I think you are going overboard, son." "But Lord, *he* started it!" So regardless of whether your offerings contribute to his salary—change his tyre. Fix her computer. Pay his phone bill. Bring her a coffee without being asked. Tell him how much his leadership is helping you move forward in your walk with God. Share the insights you receive. Never pass up a chance to be a blessing.

Most of the time, leaders know more than those they lead. I once did outdoor rock climbing with one of my pastors and his life group. I learned some amazing life application lessons that day, completely by accident. Adventure therapy, anyone? I'm a little afraid of heights, but the harnesses looked strong, nobody had injuries, the people had a can-do attitude, and it didn't look terribly hard. So up I went. Well. I quickly learned that there's a great deal of security in knowing that people are holding your line. You really do need someone, more often than you like, to tell you where your next optimal handhold is. They can see things you can't see, and while they behold the Big Picture, they're completely with you in your Small Picture. You have to trust them. You have to trust the system they've put in place. None of that is easy. And your muscles do stretch. But oh, the sense of accomplishment, and the sense of being upheld! The best line-holders don't just call out instructions. They shout up encouragement. "You're almost there! You

Their heart's desire is to help you succeed.

can reach it! You're doing great!" You are not alone. These people do not laugh at you and they do not want you to fall. Their heart's desire is to help you succeed, and to succeed with you. If you lose your grip and come off the face, they will guide your descent so you don't hurt yourself as you land.

Never underestimate, by the way, the things God can teach you through unchurched people. Just because they aren't yet redeemed doesn't mean God hasn't given them wisdom, or can't speak through them. You'll know if it's off-base. Sometimes, though, they'll hit the nail on the head. At the very least, let them tell you honestly how Churchianity strikes them—you'll get valuable feedback on how to do community engagement effectively. Let them love you. Love them back.

For that matter, let God love you. As I mentioned in Chapter 4, sometimes we get this idea that once you're saved, "you're in the army now, son." We try desperately to get people to fall in love with Jesus, and then once they are ready to acknowledge Him as boss and rescuer, their forward progress is less about enjoying this new relationship, and more about desperately trying to get *more* people to fall in love with Jesus. When we take this approach, what we're in fact doing is stripping the Bride of her wedding dress and telling her that now, she is not a preciously-cherished newlywed, but merely a baby factory, and she should go into production immediately! The irony of this is that every new wife *is* ready to rave about her bridegroom, if only she is given enough breathing room to behold, admire, interact with and receive from him. And this smittenness does indeed often result in proliferation. But if we take the Bride's focus off the Groom and put it solely on recruitment, she's got nothing to rave about except the glories of the heavenly future. She hasn't got a *now*. And all relationships founder if all they have is the past or the future and there isn't any currency.

Don't get me wrong. Evangelism and influence are of paramount importance. I'm just noting that we can't replace the horse completely with the cart. As the saying goes, the Holy Spirit is *in* you for you, and *on* you for others. It cannot, should not, must not be *for others only*. Once we stop beholding Jesus, representing Him means less and less to us. And if all we're representing is a cycle of recruitment, rather than a call to stand in awe beside us as we stand in awe of the most beautiful soul the universe knows, what we've got isn't a kingdom, but a hamster wheel. I don't know about you, but I'm not willing to give my life for a hamster wheel. And I'm certainly not willing to advertise it.

You are not just your function. You are a dearly-loved child of God. The love of God is for your life, too, not only for the lives of others: the value of a single human soul extends to yours. Preaching families of the past have been so Heaven-bent on "winning the lost" that they have failed to take into account that they might *become* "the lost". I believe this is a large part of why so many PKs and MKs leave the faith. We are so busy being other-focused—sharing the love of God with the uninitiated—that we lose sight of the fact that we are ourselves loved and eligible for all the riches there are in Christ. It might not be "all about you" but *some of it* is allowed to be about you. The love of God is not a plate of goodies set aside at a party with the screeched admonishment, "Those are for the guests!" The table is for you, too—or else every single one of us becomes ineligible the moment we actually approach. Again, you may be blessed to be a blessing, but you are also blessed because you are thoroughly loved. It all cycles together. We love because He first loved us. And having been so loved, we love Him

---

The love of God is for your life, too, not only for the lives of others.

back. Having loved Him back, we learn to love what He loves and we extend His love on. And He loves us for it. It's the cirrrrrcle of looooove!

You cannot remove from that circle the love God has for you, or the circle collapses. You are more than a conduit. Let yourself be loved. God is love, and love burns to bless. People who believe God's blessing will only ever touch them in the process of bouncing off them to someone else, don't really believe He loves them. Conversely, people who believe God's blessing is *their* birthright and everyone else should go get their own, don't really believe God loves others. The circle must cycle.

This extends to your volunteer team, too. In their hurry to be self-effacing, don't let them miss out on the blessings of God, especially mandated blessings such as the Sabbath. By that I mean, remember that while pastoral staff might get Mondays off after their massive efforts on Sunday, volunteers don't. Their efforts might be just as massive, even just as anointing-heavy, but most of them have to go to work on Monday, some of them for six days a week. Don't let them burn out in the name of "being a team player" by asking them to overcommit. "Let us not become weary in doing good" could, just possibly and additionally, mean "don't wear yourselves out; for Heaven's sake, pace yourselves!"

Talk to the Holy Spirit. Ask Him to help you run your race with diligence but also with balance. Pacing oneself is just as much a discipline as working out. Go for the long haul. Ask Him to help you equip your people to last the distance. Ask Him to help you share their shoes and their lives, their victories and their loads. One of the things Jesus chipped the professionals for was their loading down of people with burdens and not helping them. It's unclear whether He was more angry about the existence of the burdens (possibly the expanded laws that overstepped the Torah) or about the fact that nobody helped the common folk with them. Because of the earlier mention of greed, it could have been a matter of their continually asking for offerings for the Temple, even down to the widow's last cent, when in fact her welfare was their responsibility and it should have been *them* giving *her* an offering! Talk to God about the best way to care for yourself and others without unnecessary burdens.

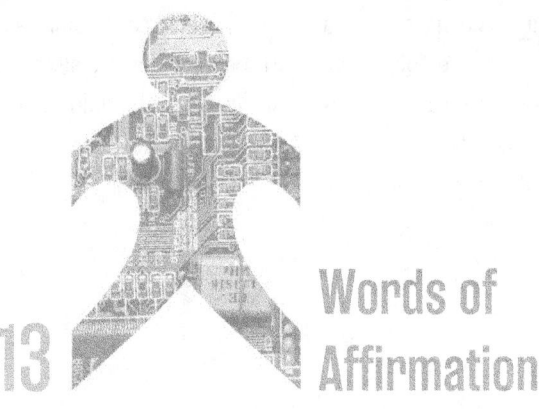

13 Words of Affirmation

AND NOW A WORD from our Sponsor. Indirectly. I hope.

You are enough. That is, He is enough and He has hand-picked you to bear His image in a specific way. So stand up straight, called one. You and God, you've got this.

You make a massive difference, and you do most of it simply by operating in love. Grace and truth together are a powerful force. Truth doesn't have to be tactless or insensitive. It's true that what is caught is deeper than what is taught. People who spend time around you are going to grow faster than people who are further away. You might even have to pick the slowest grower and hang out with them. But never doubt that you make a difference.

The leaders I've valued most in my life have been people who do empathy well. They have not minimised my suffering, nor pandered to my whining, but have taken time to step into my world and cast a look around. They've valued me not for my successes or capabilities, but for my humanity, even when I've wanted to hide the latter behind the former. On days when I've felt like an epileptic octopus in a room full of perfectly round beach balls, they've assured me I belong and am wanted. I know they won't quit believing that God is working in my life.

Words of Affirmation

Leader, for every critic, there's a fan whose life has been turned around because you were obedient to the call of God. God speaks through your words, and He speaks between them, and He speaks through your life and love. You move people forward. You help them through the maze. You let them know they're not alone. You hold out hope.

You don't have to be perfect to do any of these things. You are a human being. In fact, when I remember my leaders are *people,* I'm able to be far less critical. You are my friends. I hope to be a faithful friend in return.

You are our heroes. And you inspire us to be heroes in our own way too. And that is leadership.

Thank you

for answering the call.

Thank you

for every time you are accepting.

Thank you

for every time you show love. I know it costs you.

Words of Affirmation

Thank you
for every time you forgive us our ignorances, betrayals and failures.

Thank you
for being surrendered to God.

Thank you
for having our backs in prayer.

Thank you
for teaching us the best things you know.

Thank you
for long days and long nights.

Thank you
for believing in us, and in God-in-us.

Thank you

for your tears, and your pain, and for getting up the next day
and doing it again, because you love God and you love us
and you both think we're worth it.

Thank you

for bearing the heartache you have to carry,
because you are privy to so much broken humanity.

Thank you

for being real people trying to make a real difference,
not because you're better than us
but because you carry a burden for us.

Thank you

for the sacrifices you make in terms of career,
privacy, pay, lifestyle, and disposable time.

Thank you

for your patience while we keep putting
one foot in front of the other on our journey.

Thank you

for all the ways you love us behind the scenes,
that we never see because you can't break confidences,
dishonour those who have dishonoured you,
or blow your own trumpet.
Forgive us when we underestimate your love
because our eyes don't see the full extent of it.

Thank you,

finally,
for being
someone to look up to.

References

Holy Bible, New International Version
Biblica, www.biblegateway.com
Except where indicated, Scripture quotations are taken from the Holy Bible, New International Version®, NIV®. Copyright © 1973, 1978, 1984, 2011 by Biblica, Inc.™ Used by permission of Zondervan. All rights reserved worldwide. www.zondervan.com The "NIV" and "New International Version" are trademarks registered in the United States Patent and Trademark Office by Biblica, Inc.™.

Holy Bible: The Message (the Bible in contemparary language).
Colorado Springs, CO: NavPress, 2005

Brontë, Charlotte **Jane Eyre.**
Bucks: Transatlantic Press, 2012

Caine, Christine, Instagram post
Retrieved August 22, 2018

Hamilton, Anne **God's Panoply**.
Brisbane: Even Before Publishing, 2013

Ellis, Paul (2018, May 2) **Are Unfruitful Branches Lifted Up?**.
Retrieved from https://escapetoreality.org/2018/05/02/are-unfruitful-branches-lifted-up/

Frost, Michael & Hirsch, Alan **The Shaping of Things to Come**.
Grand Rapids: Baker Books, 2013

Johnson, David & Van Vonderen, Jeffrey **The Subtle Power of Spiritual Abuse**.
Winnipeg: Media Production Services Unit, Manitoba Educaiton, 2010

Lawrenz, Mel (2018, August 6). **The Willow Creek Crisis—Time of Reckoning for All Leaders**.
Retrieved from https://www.thebrooknetwork.org/2018/08/06/the-willow-creek-crisis-time-of-reckoning-for-all-leaders/

Lee, Morgan & Denhollander, Rachel, **My Larry Nassar Testimony Went Viral. But There's More to the Gospel Than Forgiveness.**
Retrieved from https://www.christianitytoday.com/ct/2018/january-web-only/rachael-denhollander-larry-nassar-forgiveness-gospel.html

Lencioni, Patrick **The Five Dysfunctions of a Team**.
San Francisco: Jossey-Bass, 2002

Lewis, C.S. **The Lion, the Witch and the Wardrobe**.
London: HarperCollins Publishers Ltd, 1950

Lewis, C.S. **The Horse And His Boy**.
London: HarperCollins Publishers Ltd, 1954

Lewis, C.S. **The Magician's Nephew**.
London: Harper Collins Publishers Ltd, 1955

Maxwell, John C. **Developing the Leader Within You**.
Nashville: T. Nelson, 1993.

Peters, Dan, Peters, Steve and Merrill, Cher **What About Christian Rock?**
Minneapolis: Bethany House Publishers, 1986

Plass, Adrian **The Sacred Diary of Adrian Plass Christian Speaker Aged 45 ¾**.
London: HarperCollins Publishers, 1996

Strong, J. **The New Strong's Expanded Exhaustive Concordance of the Bible.**
Nashville: Thomas Nelson, 2010

www.ingramcontent.com/pod-product-compliance
Lightning Source LLC
Chambersburg PA
CBHW071923290426
44110CB00013B/1457